CC℠ Certified
in Cybersecurity
Study Guide

CC^{SM} Certified in Cybersecurity
Study Guide

Mike Chapple, CISSP, CCSP

SYBEX®
A Wiley Brand

ACKNOWLEDGMENTS

Books like this involve work from many people, and as an author, I truly appreciate the hard work and dedication that the team at Wiley shows. I would especially like to thank my acquisitions editor, Jim Minatel. I've worked with Jim for too many years to count, and it's always an absolute pleasure working with a true industry pro.

I also greatly appreciate the editing and production team for the book, including Kelly Talbot, the project editor, who brought years of experience and great talent to the project; and Shahla Pirnia, the technical editor, who provided insightful advice and gave wonderful feedback throughout the book. I would also like to thank the many behind-the-scenes contributors, including the graphics, production, and technical teams who make the book and companion materials into a finished product.

My agent, Carole Jelen of Waterside Productions, continues to provide me with wonderful opportunities, advice, and assistance throughout my writing career.

Finally, I would like to thank my family, who supported me through the late evenings, busy weekends, and long hours that a book like this requires to write, edit, and get to press.

About the Author

Mike Chapple, CISSP, CCSP, is an author of the best-selling *CISSP (ISC)² Certified Information Systems Security Professional Official Study Guide* (Sybex, 2021), now in its ninth edition. He is an information security professional with 25 years of experience in higher education, the private sector, and government.

Mike currently serves as Teaching Professor of IT, Analytics, and Operations at the University of Notre Dame's Mendoza College of Business. He previously served as Senior Director for IT Service Delivery at Notre Dame, where he oversaw the information security, data governance, IT architecture, project management, strategic planning, and product management functions for the university.

Before returning to Notre Dame, Mike served as Executive Vice President and Chief Information Officer of the Brand Institute, a Miami-based marketing consultancy. Mike also spent four years in the information security research group at the National Security Agency and served as an active-duty intelligence officer in the U.S. Air Force.

He is a technical editor for *Information Security Magazine* and has written more than 30 books, including *Cyberwarfare: Information Operations in a Connected World* (Jones & Bartlett, 2022), *ISC2 CISSP Official Study Guide* (Wiley, 2021), and *CompTIA Cybersecurity Analyst+ (CySA+) Study Guide* (Wiley, 2023) and *Practice Tests* (Wiley, 2023).

Mike earned both his BS and PhD degrees from Notre Dame in computer science and engineering. He also holds an MS in computer science from the University of Idaho and an MBA from Auburn University. His IT certifications include the CC, CISSP, Security+, CySA+, CISA, PenTest+, CIPP/US, CISM, CCSP, and PMP credentials.

Mike provides books, video-based training, and free study groups for a wide variety of IT certifications at his website, `CertMike.com`.

About the Technical Editor

Shahla Pirnia is a freelance technical editor and proofreader with a focus on cybersecurity and certification topics.

Starting her career at Montgomery College's computer labs, Shahla quickly acquired a foundational grasp of technology in her role as a Student Aide. This foundational experience set the stage for subsequent roles: She managed a childcare provider database for a referral agency for 5 years, and then spent 9 years with a document conversion bureau. Shahla later ventured into clerical temp roles via a staffing agency and freelance writing for a digital content company.

Shahla currently serves as a technical editor for `CertMike.com`, where she works on projects including books, video courses, and practice tests.

Shahla earned BS degrees in computer and information science and psychology from the University of Maryland Global Campus, coupled with an AA degree in information systems from Montgomery College, Maryland. Shahla's IT certifications include the ISC2 Certified in Cybersecurity and the CompTIA Security+, Network+, and A+ credentials.

CONTENTS AT A GLANCE

CONTENTS

INTRODUCTION

If you're preparing to take the Certified in Cybersecurity (CC) exam, you'll undoubtedly want to find as much information as you can about information security. The more information you have at your disposal, the better off you'll be when attempting the exam. This study guide was written with that in mind. The goal is to provide enough information to prepare you for the test, but not so much that you'll be overloaded with information that's outside the scope of the exam.

This book presents the material at an entry level. You don't need any prior experience with cybersecurity to read this book or take the exam. The CC certification is designed for newcomers to the field, and this book will give you all the information you need to know to pass it.

I've included review questions at the end of each chapter to give you a taste of what it's like to take the exam. I recommend that you check out these questions first to gauge your level of expertise. You can then use the book mainly to fill in the gaps in your current knowledge. This study guide will help you round out your knowledge base before tackling the exam.

If you can answer the review questions correctly for a given chapter, you can feel safe moving on to the next chapter. If you're unable to answer them correctly, reread the chapter and try the questions again. Your score should improve.

> **NOTE**
>
> Don't just study the questions and answers! The questions on the actual exam will be different from the practice questions included in this book. The exam is designed to test your knowledge of a concept or objective, so use this book to learn the objectives behind the questions.

CC CERTIFICATION

The CC certification is offered by the International Information System Security Certification Consortium, or ISC2, a global nonprofit organization. The mission of ISC2 is to support and provide members and constituents with credentials, resources, and leadership to address cyber, information, software, and infrastructure security to deliver value to society. ISC2 achieves this mission by delivering the world's leading information security certification program. The CC is the flagship credential in this series and is accompanied by several other ISC2 programs:

▶ Certified Information Systems Security Professional (CISSP)
▶ Systems Security Certified Practitioner (SSCP)
▶ Certified Secure Software Lifecycle Professional (CSSLP)
▶ Certified Cloud Security Professional (CCSP)
▶ Certified in Governance, Risk, and Compliance (CGRC)

The CC certification covers five domains of information security knowledge. These domains are meant to serve as the broad knowledge foundation required to succeed in the information security profession:

▶ Security Principles (26% of exam questions)
▶ Business Continuity (BC), Disaster Recovery (DR) & Incident Response (IR) Concepts (10% of exam questions)
▶ Access Control Concepts (22% of exam questions)
▶ Network Security (24% of exam questions)
▶ Security Operations (18% of exam questions)

Complete details about the CC exam objectives are contained in the Exam Outline. It includes a full outline of exam topics and can be found on the ISC2 website at www.isc2.org/Certifications/cc/cc-certification-exam-outline.

TAKING THE CC EXAM

The CC exam includes only standard multiple-choice questions. Each question has four possible answers, and only one of the answers is correct. When taking the test, you'll likely find some questions where you think multiple answers might be correct. In those cases, remember that you're looking for the *best* possible answer to the question!

The CC exam is currently available for free to the first one million candidates through an ISC2 initiative called One Million Certified in Cybersecurity. You can find more details about the CC exam and how to take it at www.isc2.org/Certifications/CC.

You'll have 2 hours to take the exam and will be asked to answer 100 questions. Your exam will be scored on a scale of 1,000 possible points, with a passing score of 700.

> **NOTE**
>
> The CC exam includes 25 unscored questions, meaning that only 75 of the questions actually count toward your score. ISC2 does this to gather research data, which it then uses when developing new versions of the exam. So, if you come across a question that does not appear to map to any of the exam objectives—or, for that matter, does not appear to belong in the exam—it is likely a seeded question. You never really know whether or not a question is seeded, however, so always make your best effort to answer every question.

COMPUTER-BASED TESTING ENVIRONMENT

The CC exam is administered in a computer-based testing (CBT) format. You can register for the exam through the ISC2 and Pearson VUE websites.

You take the exam in a Pearson VUE testing center located near your home or office. The centers administer many different exams, so you may find yourself sitting in the same room as a student taking a school entrance examination and a health care professional earning a medical certification. If you'd like to become more familiar with the testing environment, the Pearson VUE website offers a virtual tour of a testing center at home.pearsonvue.com/ test-taker/Pearson-Professional-Center-Tour.aspx.

When you take the exam, you'll be seated at a computer that has the exam software already loaded and running. It's a pretty straightforward interface that allows you to navigate through the exam. You can download a practice exam and tutorial from the Pearson VUE website at www.vue.com/athena/athena.asp.

> **EXAM TIP**
>
> At the beginning of the exam, you'll be asked to agree to the terms. This section of the exam has its own 5-minute timer. If you don't agree within 5 minutes, your exam will automatically end and you will not be able to restart it!

EXAM RETAKE POLICY

If you don't pass the CC exam, you shouldn't panic. Many individuals don't reach the bar on their first attempt but gain valuable experience that helps them succeed the second time around. When retaking the exam, you'll have the benefit of familiarity with the CBT environment and CC exam format. You'll also have time to study the areas where you felt less confident.

After your first exam attempt, you must wait 30 days before retaking it. If you're not successful on that attempt, you must then wait 60 days before your third attempt and 90 days before your fourth attempt. You cannot take the exam more than three times in a single calendar year.

RECERTIFICATION REQUIREMENTS

Once you've earned your CC credential, you'll need to maintain your certification by paying maintenance fees and participating in continuing professional education (CPE). As long as you maintain your certification in good standing, you will not need to retake the CC exam.

Currently, the annual maintenance fee for the CC credential is $50 for those who do not hold another ISC2 certification. Members who hold another credential pay a $125 maintenance fee each year. This fee covers the renewal for all ISC2 certifications held by an individual.

The CC CPE requirement mandates earning at least 45 CPE credits during each three-year renewal cycle. ISC2 provides an online portal where certificate holders can submit CPE completion for review and approval. The portal also tracks annual maintenance fee payments and progress toward recertification.

USING THE ONLINE PRACTICE TEST

All the questions in this book are also available in Sybex's online practice test tool, along with a full-length 100-question CC practice test. To get access to this online format, go to www.wiley.com/go/sybextestprep and start by registering your book. You'll receive a PIN code and instructions on where to create an online test bank account. Once you have access, you can use the online version to create your own sets of practice tests from the book questions and practice in a timed and graded setting.

In addition to the questions and practice test, the Sybex online learning environment includes an extensive set of electronic flashcards to improve your exam preparation. Each flashcard has one question and one correct answer. These are great as last minute drills. And there is an online glossary is a searchable list of key terms introduced in this study guide that you should know for the CC certification exam.

HOW TO CONTACT THE PUBLISHER

If you believe you have found a mistake in this book, please bring it to our attention. At John Wiley & Sons, we understand how important it is to provide our customers with accurate content, but even with our best efforts an error may occur.

In order to submit your possible errata, please email it to our Customer Service Team at wileysupport@wiley.com with the subject line "Possible Book Errata Submission."

PART I

Domain 1: Security Principles

Chapter 1 Confidentiality, Integrity, Availability, and Non-repudiation
Chapter 2 Authentication and Authorization
Chapter 3 Privacy
Chapter 4 Risk Management
Chapter 5 Security Controls
Chapter 6 Ethics
Chapter 7 Security Governance Processes

Security Principles is the first domain of ISC2's Certified in Cybersecurity exam. It provides the foundational knowledge that anyone in information technology needs to understand as they begin their careers. The domain includes the following five objectives:

1.1 **Understand the security concepts of information assurance**
1.2 **Understand the risk management process**
1.3 **Understand security controls**
1.4 **Understand the ISC2 Code of Ethics**
1.5 **Understand governance processes**

Questions from this domain make up 26 percent of the questions on the CC exam, so you should expect to see 26 questions on your test covering the material in this part.

CHAPTER 1

Confidentiality, Integrity, Availability, and Non-repudiation

Objective 1.1 Understand the Security Concepts of Information Assurance

Information plays a vital role in the operations of modern business, and we find ourselves entrusted with sensitive information about our customers, employees, internal operations, and other critical matters. As information technology professionals, we must work with information security teams, other technology professionals, and business leaders to protect the security of that information.

In this chapter, you'll learn about four of the subobjectives of CC objective 1.1. The remaining material for this objective is covered in Chapter 2, "Authentication and Authorization," and Chapter 3, "Privacy." The following subobjectives are covered in this chapter:

▶ Confidentiality
▶ Integrity
▶ Availability
▶ Non-repudiation

THE CIA TRIAD

Cybersecurity professionals have three primary objectives when it comes to protecting information and systems. They want to ensure that private data remains secret (confidentiality), that information isn't altered without permission (integrity), and that information is available to authorized users when they need it (availability). You can remember these three main goals by thinking of the CIA triad, as shown in Figure 1.1. Each side of this triangle covers one of the three main goals.

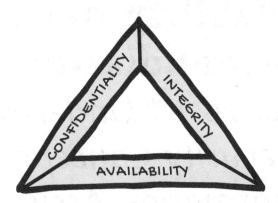

FIGURE 1.1 The CIA triad summarizes the three main goals of information security: confidentiality, integrity, and availability.

Confidentiality

Confidentiality ensures that only authorized individuals have access to information and resources. This is what most people think of when they think about information security—keeping secrets away from prying eyes. And it is, in fact, how security professionals spend the majority of their time.

Confidentiality Risks

As you prepare for the exam, you'll need to understand the main threats against each of the cybersecurity objectives. I'll talk about many different kinds of threats in this book, but I'll begin with the following: snooping, dumpster diving, eavesdropping, wiretapping, and social engineering.

Snooping   *Snooping* is exactly what the name implies. The individual engaging in snooping wanders around your office or other facility and simply looks to see what information they can gather. When people leave sensitive papers on their desks or in a public area, it creates an opportunity for snooping.

Organizations can protect against snooping by enforcing a clean desk policy. Employees should maintain a clean workspace and put away any sensitive materials whenever they step away, even if it's just for a moment.

Dumpster Diving   *Dumpster diving* attacks also look for sensitive materials, but the attacker doesn't walk around the office; instead, they look through the trash, trying to find sensitive documents that an employee threw in the garbage or recycling bin.

You can protect your organization against dumpster diving attacks using a simple piece of technology: a paper shredder! If you destroy documents before discarding them, you'll protect against a dumpster diver pulling them out of the trash.

Eavesdropping   *Eavesdropping* attacks come in both physical and electronic types. In a physical eavesdropping attack, the attacker simply positions themselves where they can overhear conversations, such as in a cafeteria or hallway, and then listens for sensitive information.

You can protect against eavesdropping attacks by putting rules in place limiting where sensitive conversations may take place. For example, sensitive conversations should generally take place in a closed office or conference room.

Electronic eavesdropping attacks are also known as *wiretapping*. They occur when an attacker gains access to a network and monitors the data being sent electronically within an office.

The best way to protect against electronic eavesdropping attacks is to use encryption to protect information being sent over the network. If data is encrypted, an attacker who intercepts that data won't be able to make any sense of it. I'll talk more about how encryption works later in this book.

Social Engineering   The last type of confidentiality attack I'll talk about is *social engineering*. In a social engineering attack, the attacker uses psychological tricks to persuade an employee to give them sensitive information or access to internal systems. They might pretend that they're on an urgent assignment from a senior leader, impersonate an IT technician, or send a phishing email.

It's difficult to protect against social engineering attacks. The best defense against these attacks is educating users to recognize the dangers of social engineering and empower them to intervene when they suspect an attack is taking place.

Integrity

Security professionals are also responsible for protecting the *integrity* of an organization's information. This means that there aren't any unauthorized changes to information. Unauthorized changes may come in the form of a hacker seeking to intentionally alter information or a service disruption accidentally affecting data stored in a system. In either case, it's the information security professional's responsibility to prevent these lapses in integrity.

Integrity Risks

This section covers four types of integrity attacks: the unauthorized modification of information, impersonation attacks, man-in-the-middle (MitM) attacks, and replay attacks.

Unauthorized Modification of Information   The unauthorized modification of information occurs when an attacker gains access to a system and makes changes that violate a security policy. This might be an external attack, such as an intruder breaking into a financial system and issuing themselves checks, or it might be an internal attack, such as an employee increasing their own salary in the payroll system.

Following the principle of *least privilege* is the best way to protect against integrity attacks. Organizations should carefully consider the permissions that each employee needs to perform their job and then limit employees to the smallest set of permissions possible.

Impersonation   In an *impersonation* attack, the attacker pretends to be someone other than who they actually are. They might impersonate a manager, executive, or IT technician in order to convince someone to change data in a system. This is an extension of the social engineering attacks mentioned earlier, and the best defense against these attacks is strong user education.

Man-in-the-Middle Attacks   Sometimes impersonation attacks are electronic. In a *man-in-the-middle (MitM) attack*, the attacker intercepts network traffic as a user is logging into a system and pretends to be that system. They then sit in the middle of the communication, relaying information between the user and the system while they monitor everything that is occurring. In this type of attack, the attacker might be able to steal a user's password and use it later to log in to the system themselves.

Replay Attacks   In a *replay attack*, the attacker doesn't get in the middle of the communication but finds a way to observe a legitimate user logging into a system. They then capture the information used to log in to the system and later replay it on the network to gain access themselves.

The best defense against both replay and MitM attacks is the use of encryption to protect communications. For example, web traffic might use the Transport Layer Security (TLS) protocol to prevent an eavesdropper from observing network traffic. You'll learn more about this technology in Chapter 18, "Encryption."

Availability

As a security professional, you must also understand how to apply security controls that protect the *availability* of information and systems. As the third leg of the CIA triad, availability controls ensure that information and systems remain available to authorized users when needed. They protect against disruptions to normal system operation or data availability.

Availability Risks

This chapter covers five different types of events that can disrupt the availability of systems: denial-of-service attacks, power outages, hardware failures, destruction of equipment, and service outages.

Denial-of-Service Attacks   *Denial-of-service (DoS) attacks* occur when a malicious individual bombards a system with an overwhelming amount of network traffic. The idea is to simply send so many requests to a server that it is unable to answer any requests from legitimate users.

You can protect your systems against DoS attacks by using firewalls that block illegitimate requests and by partnering with your Internet service provider to block DoS attacks before they reach your network.

Power Outages   Power outages can occur on a local or regional level for many different reasons. Increased demand can overwhelm the power grid; natural disasters can disrupt service; and other factors can cause power outages that disrupt access to systems.

You can protect against power outages by having redundant power sources and backup generators that supply power to your system when commercial power is not available.

Hardware Failures   Hardware failures can and do occur. Servers, hard drives, network gear, and other equipment all fail occasionally and can disrupt access to information. That's an availability problem.

You can protect against hardware failures by building a system that has built-in redundancy so that if one component fails, another is ready to pick up the slack.

Destruction of Equipment   Sometimes equipment is just outright destroyed. This might be the result of intentional or accidental physical damage, or it may be the result of a larger disaster, such as a fire or a hurricane.

You can protect against small-scale destruction with redundant systems. If you want to protect against larger-scale disasters, you may need to have backup data centers in remote locations or in the cloud that can keep running when your primary data center is disrupted.

Service Outages   Finally, sometimes service outages occur. This might be due to programming errors, the failure of underlying equipment, or many other reasons. These outages disrupt user access to systems and information and are, therefore, an availability concern.

You can protect against service outages by building systems that are resilient in the face of errors and hardware failures.

NON-REPUDIATION

Another important focus of some security controls is providing *non-repudiation*. Repudiation is a term that means denying that something is true. Non-repudiation is a security goal that prevents someone from falsely denying that something is true.

For example, you might agree to pay someone $10,000 in exchange for a car. If you just had a handshake agreement, it might be possible for you to later repudiate your actions. You might claim that you never agreed to purchase the car or that you agreed to pay a lower price.

To solve this issue, a signed contract is used when a car is sold. Your signature on the document is the proof that you agreed to the terms, and if you later go to court, the person selling you the car can prove that you agreed by showing the judge the signed document. Physical signatures provide non-repudiation on contracts, receipts, and other paper documents.

There's also an electronic form of the physical signature. *Digital signatures* use encryption technology to provide non-repudiation for electronic documents. You'll learn more about that technology in Chapter 18.

There are other ways that you can provide non-repudiation as well. You might use biometric security controls, such as a fingerprint or facial recognition, to prove that someone was in a facility or performed an action. You might also use video surveillance for that same purpose. All of these controls enable you to prove that someone was in a particular location or performed an action, offering some degree of non-repudiation.

EXAM ESSENTIALS

▶ The CIA triad references the three main goals of information security: confidentiality, integrity, and availability.

▶ Confidentiality protects sensitive information from unauthorized access. The major threats to confidentiality include snooping, dumpster diving, eavesdropping, wiretapping, and social engineering.

▶ Integrity protects information and systems from unauthorized modification. The major threats to integrity include the unauthorized modification of information, impersonation attacks, man-in-the-middle attacks, and replay attacks.

▶ Availability ensures that authorized users have access to information when they need it. The major threats to availability include denial-of-service attacks, power outages, hardware failures, destruction of equipment, and service outages.

▶ Non-repudiation uses technical measures to ensure that a user is not able to later deny that they took some action.

Practice Question 1

Which one of the following security risks would most likely be considered an availability issue?

A. Replay attack
B. Power outage
C. Social engineering
D. Snooping

Practice Question 2

What are the three major objectives of cybersecurity programs?

A. Confidentiality, integrity, and availability
B. Confidentiality, integrity, and authorization
C. Confidentiality, infrastructure, and authorization
D. Communications, infrastructure, and authorization

Practice Question 1 Explanation

Availability issues affect the ability of authorized users to gain access to information, systems, or other resources that they need. All of the issues listed here are cybersecurity risks that you need to be aware of when you take the CC exam, but only power outages are classified as an availability risk. This is because a power outage can easily disrupt access to systems and information by causing those systems to be offline.

Replay attacks allow an unauthorized individual to impersonate a legitimate user and are primarily considered integrity risks.

Social engineering and snooping attacks may allow an attacker to gain access to sensitive information and are primarily considered confidentiality risks.

Correct Answer: B. Power outage

Practice Question 2 Explanation

The three major objectives of any cybersecurity program are protecting the confidentiality, integrity, and availability of systems and information.

Confidentiality ensures that only authorized individuals have access to information and resources. Integrity protects information from unauthorized changes. Availability ensures that information and systems are available for authorized use.

Correct Answer: A. Confidentiality, integrity, and availability

CHAPTER 2

Authentication and Authorization

Objective 1.1 Understand the Security Concepts of Information Assurance

As an IT professional, one of the most important things you do is to ensure that only authorized individuals gain access to information, systems, and networks under your protection. You use access controls to provide this assurance.

In this chapter, you'll learn about the fourth subobjective of CC objective 1.1. The remaining material for this objective is covered in Chapter 1, "Confidentiality, Integrity, Availability, and Non-repudiation," and Chapter 3, "Privacy." The following subobjective is covered in this chapter:

▶ **Authentication (e.g., methods of authentication, multi-factor authentication (MFA))**

ACCESS CONTROL PROCESS

The access control process consists of three steps that you must understand as you prepare for the Certified in Cybersecurity (CC) exam: identification, authentication, and authorization. Access control systems also perform another important task: accounting.

> **EXAM TIP**
>
> Together, the activities performed by an access control system are referred to as AAA, or "triple-A." Those three As are for authentication, authorization, and accounting. Yes, that leaves identification off the list, but identification is assumed to be part of the process if you're performing authentication, and adding an "I" would ruin the easy acronym!

Identification

During the first step of the process, *identification*, an individual makes a claim about their identity. The person trying to gain access doesn't present any proof at this point; they simply make an assertion. It's important to remember that the identification step is only a claim, and the user could certainly be making a false claim! Imagine a physical-world scenario in which you want to enter a secure office building where you have an appointment. During the identification step of the process, you might walk up to the security desk and say, "Hi, I'm Mike Chapple."

Authentication

Proof comes into play during the second step of the process: *authentication*. During the authentication step, the individual proves their identity to the satisfaction of the access control system. In the office building example, the guard would likely want to see my driver's license to confirm my identity.

Authorization

Just proving your identity isn't enough to gain access to a system, however. The access control system also needs to be satisfied that you are *allowed* to access the system. That's the third step of the access control process: *authorization*. In the office building example, the security guard might check a list of that day's appointments to see if it includes my name.

Accounting

In addition to identification, authentication, and authorization, access control systems also provide an *accounting* functionality that allows administrators to track user activity and reconstruct it from logs. In the case of the office building example, the security guard may write down my access to the building in a visitor logbook. Figure 2.1 shows this process all coming together.

Digital Access Control

So far, I've talked about identification, authentication, authorization, and accounting in the context of gaining access to a building. Now I'll discuss how they work in the electronic world. When we log in to a system, we most often identify ourselves using a username, most likely composed of some combination of the letters from our names. When we reach the authentication phase, we're commonly asked to enter a password.

> **NOTE**
> There are many other ways to authenticate, and I'll talk about those later in this chapter. I'll also discuss how strong access control systems combine multiple authentication approaches.

FIGURE 2.1 The physical access control process

In the electronic world, authorization often takes the form of *access control lists* that itemize the specific file system permissions granted to an individual user or a group of users. Users proceed through identification, authentication, and authorization when they request access to a resource.

Digital systems also perform a significant amount of accounting. This may include tracking user activity on systems and even logging user web browsing history. Any tracking that takes place as part of an organization's monitoring program should fit within the boundaries set by the law and the organization's privacy policy.

Figure 2.2 shows the digital access control process coming together.

PASSWORD POLICIES

When you set a password policy for your organization, you have a number of technical controls available that allow you to set requirements for how users choose and maintain their passwords. This section discusses a few of those mechanisms.

FIGURE 2.2 The digital access control process

Password Length

The simplest and most common control on passwords is setting the *password length*. This is simply the minimum number of characters that must be included in a password. It's good practice to require that passwords be at least eight characters, but some organizations require even longer passwords. The longer a password is, the harder it is to guess.

Password Complexity

Organizations may also set *password complexity* requirements. These requirements force users to include different types of characters in their passwords, such as uppercase and lowercase letters, digits, and special characters. Just as with password length, the more character types there are in a password, the harder it is to guess.

Password Expiration

Password expiration requirements force users to change their passwords periodically. For example, an organization might set a password expiration period of 180 days, forcing users to change their passwords every 6 months. These days, many organizations no longer have password expiration requirements, allowing users to keep the same password for as long as they'd like and only requiring that they change it if the password is compromised.

Password History

Password history requirements are designed to prevent users from reusing old passwords. Organizations with password history requirements configure their systems to remember the previous passwords used by each user and prevent them from reusing that password in the future. Password history controls allow the administrator to identify how many old passwords are remembered for each user.

Password Resets

Every organization should allow users to change their passwords quickly and easily. You want users to be able to privately select their own passwords and do so whenever they are concerned that their password may be compromised.

One point of caution is that organizations should carefully evaluate their password reset process for users who forget their passwords. If they're not designed well, these processes can provide an opportunity for attackers to gain access to a system by performing an unauthorized password reset.

Password Reuse

IT teams should also strongly encourage users not to reuse the same password across multiple sites. This is difficult to actually enforce, but it does provide a strong measure of security. If a user reuses the same password on many different sites and one of those sites is compromised, an attacker might test that password on other sites, hoping that the password owner reuses the same password.

Password Managers

It's difficult for users to manage unique passwords for every site they visit. That's where password managers play a crucial role. These valuable tools are secure password vaults, often protected by biometric security mechanisms that create and store unique passwords. They then automatically fill those passwords on websites when the user visits them. That way users can have unique, strong passwords for every site they visit without having to remember them all.

Figure 2.3 shows an example of LastPass, a popular password manager, being used to create a new, strong password.

F I G U R E 2 . 3 **Creating a password in LastPass**

AUTHENTICATION FACTORS

Computer systems offer many different authentication techniques that allow users to prove their identity. This section looks at the following three authentication factors:

- ▶ Something you know
- ▶ Something you are
- ▶ Something you have

Something You Know

By far, the most common authentication factor is *something you know*. I've already talked about how passwords are the most commonly used authentication technique. This is a "something you know" factor because the password is something that the user remembers and enters into a system during the authentication process. Personal identification numbers (PINs) and the answers to security questions are also examples of something you know.

Something You Are

The second authentication factor is *something you are*. *Biometric* authentication techniques measure one of your physical characteristics, such as a fingerprint, eye pattern, face, or voice. Figure 2.4 shows an example of a smartphone fingerprint reader performing biometric authentication.

Figure 2.5 shows a more complex eye scan being performed as a biometric access control for entering a facility.

FIGURE 2.4 **Fingerprint authentication on a smartphone**
Source: artiemedvedev/Adobe Stock Photos

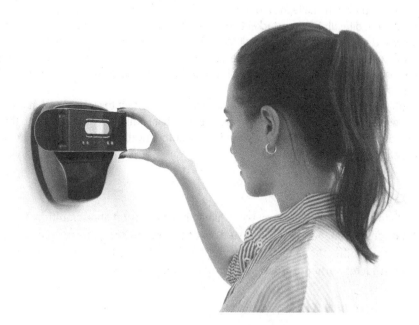

FIGURE 2.5 **Eye scan authentication for entering a facility**
Source: demphoto/Adobe Stock Photos

Something You Have

The third authentication factor, *something you have*, requires the user to have physical possession of a device, such as a smartphone running a software token application or a hardware authentication token key fob. These devices generate onetime passwords that are displayed to the user and allow them to prove that they have access to a physical device. Similarly, smart cards can serve as a "something you have" factor, requiring that the user insert a card with a digital chip into a specialized reader.

Multi-factor Authentication

When used alone, any one of these techniques provides some security for systems. However, they each have their own drawbacks. For example, an attacker might steal a user's password through a phishing attack. Once they have the password, they can then use that password to assume the user's identity. Other authentication factors aren't foolproof either. If you use smart card authentication to implement something you have, the user may lose the smart card. Someone coming across it may then impersonate the user.

The solution to this problem is to combine authentication techniques from multiple factors, such as combining something you know with something you have. This approach is known as *multi-factor authentication (MFA)*.

Take the two techniques just discussed: passwords and smart cards. When used alone, either one is subject to attackers gaining knowledge of the password or stealing a smart card. However, if an authentication system requires both a password (something you know) and a smart card (something you have), it brings added security. If the hacker steals the password, they don't have the required smart card, and vice versa. It suddenly becomes much more difficult for the attacker to gain access to the account. Because something you know and something you have are different factors, this is multi-factor authentication.

You can combine other factors as well. For example, a fingerprint reader (something you are) might also require the entry of a PIN (something you know). That's another example of multi-factor authentication.

When evaluating multi-factor authentication, it's important to remember that the techniques must be *different* factors. An approach that combines a password with the answer to a security question is *not* multi-factor authentication, because both factors are something you know.

EXAM TIP

When you take the CC exam, you'll likely find a question about multi-factor authentication. Be careful to ensure that the authentication techniques come from two different factors. Mistaking two "something you know" techniques for multi-factor authentication is a common exam mistake!

EXAM ESSENTIALS

▶ The access control process consists of three major steps. Identification is when a user makes a claim of identity. Authentication is when the user proves that identity claim. Authorization is when the system determines whether the user is allowed to perform a requested action.

▶ Accounting processes create a record of who performed which actions on a system and are useful when investigating security incidents.

▶ Multi-factor authentication combines at least two of the three factors: something you know, something you have, and something you are.

▶ Password length requirements set a minimum number of characters that must be in a user's password, whereas password complexity requirements mandate the use of different character types.

▶ Password history requirements prevent the reuse of old passwords, whereas password expiration requirements force the periodic reset of existing passwords. Users should be permitted to reset their passwords whenever they wish.

▶ Users should be encouraged not to reuse passwords across multiple sites, as this increases the risk of compromise. Password managers provide a convenient tool for managing many unique, strong passwords.

Practice Question 1

You are considering deploying a multi-factor authentication system to protect access to your organization's virtual private network (VPN). Which one of the following combinations of access controls would meet this requirement?

A. Password and PIN
B. Fingerprint and eye scan
C. Smart card and fingerprint
D. Key fob and smart card

Practice Question 2

Andy is attempting to change his password and has created the following long password:

p7djkqnr2LAD

He receives an error message that he must use a symbol in his password. Which password policy is he failing to meet?

A. Password length
B. Password history
C. Password complexity
D. Password reuse

Practice Question 1 Explanation

Before you can answer this question, you must identify the authentication factors in use here.

Passwords and PINs are both examples of something you know.

Fingerprint and eye scan are both examples of something you are.

Key fobs and smart cards are both examples of something you have.

The only answer option that combines techniques from two different factors is the use of a smart card (something you have) with a fingerprint (something you are).

Correct Answer: C. Smart card and fingerprint

Practice Question 2 Explanation

This is an example of a password complexity requirement. The message is requiring that Andy use a symbol in his password, and password complexity requirements require the use of different character types.

There is no indication that Andy is attempting to reuse an old password, which would violate a password history or reuse requirement. There is also no indication that his password is too short and does not meet the password length requirements.

Correct Answer: C. Password complexity

CHAPTER 3

Privacy

Objective 1.1 Understand the Security Concepts of Information Assurance

In the digital era, the organizations we deal with collect a lot of information about individuals and their actions. From credit card transactions to educational records, each of us generates a significant trail of data, and we are rightfully concerned about the *privacy* of that information.

In this chapter, you'll learn about the sixth subobjective of CC objective 1.1. The remaining material for this objective is covered in Chapter 1, "Confidentiality, Integrity, Availability, and Non-repudiation," and Chapter 2, "Authentication and Authorization." The following subobjective is covered in this chapter:

▶ **Privacy**

PRIVACY

As a cybersecurity professional, you have a few interests in how organizations collect and use personal information:

▶ You are obviously concerned about the privacy of your own personal information.

▶ You have a responsibility to educate the users in your organization about how they can protect their own personal information.

▶ You have a responsibility to assist the privacy officials within your organization with the work they need to do to protect the personal information entrusted to your organization.

Types of Private Information

Private information may come in many forms. Two of the most common elements of private information are personally identifiable information and protected health information:

► *Personally identifiable information (PII)* includes all information that can be tied back to a specific individual.

► *Protected health information (PHI)* includes health care records that are regulated under the Health Insurance Portability and Accountability Act (HIPAA).

Expectation of Privacy

Privacy programs are based on a legal principle known as the *reasonable expectation of privacy*. Many laws that govern whether information must be protected are based on whether the person disclosing the information had a reasonable expectation of privacy when they did so and whether the disclosure would violate that reasonable expectation of privacy.

When you put content on social media, whether it be a post on a social networking site or a comment on a shared video, you generally have no reasonable expectation of privacy. You're posting that content publicly or to a large group of people, and a reasonable person would assume that is not a private conversation.

However, when you send a message to someone over email or instant messaging, or share a file through a file sharing site with a specific person or small group, you do have an expectation of privacy. If you don't encrypt the message, you do run the risk that others will eavesdrop on the message, but you have a more reasonable expectation of privacy.

At the other end of the spectrum, when you provide private information to a government agency through their website, such as completing your taxes or registering for a medical insurance program, you have a much greater expectation of privacy. In those cases, you expect that the agency collecting information will treat that information with care and not share it without your permission. And, in fact, most countries have laws that require this information be kept private.

When you're using a computer or network that belongs to your employer, you generally do not have a reasonable expectation of privacy. The employer owns that equipment and is normally legally entitled to monitor the use of their systems. If you're using software on your employer's desktop computer, accessing business information over a corporate network, or even using the Internet at work for personal use, you generally should not expect to have privacy for your communication.

As a cybersecurity professional, you should communicate to users clearly and accurately about their privacy expectations. It's important to reinforce that when employees of your organization are using systems or networks that belong to the organization, they should not have an expectation of privacy. Figure 3.1 illustrates cases where users do and do not have a reasonable expectation of privacy.

You also need to ensure that you and your organization are appropriately handling confidential information. In addition to protecting personal information about employees and customers, you should take steps to safeguard other sensitive information, including passwords and the company's confidential information.

FIGURE 3.1 Do you have a reasonable expectation of privacy?

PRIVACY MANAGEMENT FRAMEWORK

The *Privacy Management Framework (PMF)* is an attempt to establish a global framework for privacy management. The PMF includes nine principles that were developed by the American Institute of Certified Public Accountants (AICPA) with subject matter expert input.

The nine PMF principles are as follows:

1. Management
2. Agreement, notice, and communication
3. Collection and creation
4. Use, retention, and disposal
5. Access
6. Disclosure to third parties
7. Security for privacy
8. Data integrity and quality
9. Monitoring and enforcement

The remainder of this section explores each of these principles in more detail.

Management

Management is the first of the nine privacy principles, and the PMF defines it as follows: "The entity defines, formally documents, communicates, and assigns accountability for its PI (personal information) privacy policies and procedures."

The criteria that organizations should follow to establish control over the management of their privacy program includes the following:

- Creating written privacy policies and communicating those policies to personnel
- Assigning responsibility and accountability for those policies to a person or team
- Establishing procedures for the review and approval of privacy policies and changes to those policies
- Ensuring that privacy policies are consistent with applicable laws and regulations
- Performing privacy risk assessments on at least an annual basis
- Ensuring that contractual obligations to customers, vendors, and partners are consistent with privacy policies
- Assessing privacy risks when implementing or changing technology infrastructure
- Creating and maintaining a privacy incident management process
- Conducting privacy awareness and training and establishing qualifications for employees with privacy responsibilities

Agreement, Notice, and Communication

The second principle, *agreement, notice, and communication*, requires that organizations inform individuals about their privacy practices and obtain agreement for information processing. The PMF defines this principle as follows: "The entity makes formal agreements, notifies and communicates with and offers choices when seeking data subject consents, including reasons why and purposes for which the entity seeks to obtain and use a data subject's PI."

The principle incorporates the following criteria:

- Including notice practices in the organization's privacy policies
- Notifying individuals about the purpose of collecting personal information and the organization's policies surrounding the other principles
- Providing notice to individuals at the time of data collection, when policies and procedures change, and when the organization intends to use information for new purposes not disclosed in earlier notices
- Writing privacy notices in plain and simple language and posting them conspicuously
- Including choice and consent practices in the organization's privacy policies
- Informing individuals about the choice and consent options available to them and the consequences of refusing to provide personal information or withdrawing consent to use personal information
- Obtaining implicit or explicit consent at or before the time that personal information is collected
- Notifying individuals of proposed new uses for previously collected information and obtaining additional consent for those new uses
- Obtaining direct explicit consent from individuals when the organization collects, uses, or discloses sensitive personal information
- Obtaining consent before transferring personal information to or from an individual's computer or device

Collection and Creation

The principle of *collection and creation* governs the ways that organizations come into the possession of personal information. The PMF defines this principle as follows: "The entity collects and creates PI only for the purposes identified in its agreements with data subjects, and in ongoing communications with and notices provided to data subjects."

The criteria associated with the collection and creation principle are as follows:

- ► Including collection practices in the organization's privacy policies
- ► Informing individuals that their personal information will be collected only for identified purposes
- ► Including details on the methods used to collect data and the types of data collected in the organization's privacy notice
- ► Collecting information using fair and lawful means and only for the purposes identified in the privacy notice
- ► Confirming that any third parties who provide the organization with personal information have collected it fairly and lawfully and that the information is reliable
- ► Informing individuals if the organization obtains additional information about them

> **NOTE**
>
> Although it is not explicitly included in the collection criteria, data minimization is another crucial component of privacy programs. This principle says that an organization should collect the minimum amount of personal information necessary to meet their objectives and discard that information when it is no longer needed for that purpose.

Use, Retention, and Disposal

Organizations must maintain the privacy of personal information throughout its life cycle. This is where the principle of *use, retention, and disposal* plays an important role. The PMF defines this principle as follows: "The entity limits the use of PI to the purposes identified in the formal agreements/notices, and for which a data subject has provided explicit (or implicit) consent. The entity retains PI for the time necessary to fulfill the stated purposes identified in the formal agreements/notices or as required by laws or regulations. Once those purposes have been met, the entity securely disposes of the information."

The criteria associated with the use, retention, and disposal principle are as follows:

- ► Including collection practices in the organization's privacy policies
- ► Informing individuals that their personal information will be used only for disclosed purposes for which the organization has obtained consent, and then abiding by that statement

▶ Informing individuals that their data will be retained for no longer than necessary, and then abiding by that statement

▶ Informing individuals that information that is no longer needed will be disposed of securely, and then abiding by that statement

Access

One of the core elements of individual privacy is the belief that individuals should have the right to access information that an organization holds about them and, when necessary, to correct that information. This right to correct information is also known as the right of redress. The PMF definition of the *access* principle is as follows: "The entity provides data subjects with access to their PI when requested or when asked to update and correct data errors or make changes."

The criteria associated with the access principle are as follows:

▶ Including practices around access to personal information in the organization's privacy policies

▶ Informing individuals about the procedures for reviewing, updating, and correcting their personal information

▶ Providing individuals with a mechanism to determine whether the organization maintains personal information about them and to review any such information

▶ Authenticating an individual's identity before providing them with access to personal information

▶ Providing access to information in an understandable format within a reasonable period of time and either for a reasonable charge that is based on the organization's actual costs or at no cost

▶ Informing individuals in writing why any requests to access or update personal information were denied and informing them of any appeal rights they may have

▶ Providing a mechanism for individuals to update or correct personal information and providing that updated information to third parties who received it from the organization

Disclosure to Third Parties

Some challenging privacy issues arise when organizations maintain personal information about an individual and then choose to share that information with third parties in the course of doing business. The PMF defines the *disclosure to third parties* principle as follows: "The entity discloses PI to third parties only for the purposes identified in data subject privacy agreements and its privacy notice and with the explicit consent of the data subject."

The criteria associated with the disclosure to third parties principle are as follows:

▶ Including third-party disclosure practices in the organization's privacy policies

▶ Informing individuals of any third-party disclosures that take place and the purpose of those disclosures

▶ Informing third parties who receive personal information from the organization that they must comply with the organization's privacy policy and
handling practices

▶ Disclosing personal information to third parties without notice or for purposes
other than those disclosed in the notice only when required to do so by law

▶ Disclosing information to third parties only under the auspices of an
agreement that the third party will protect the information consistent with the
organization's privacy policy

▶ Implementing procedures designed to verify that the privacy controls of third
parties receiving personal information from the organization are functioning
effectively

▶ Taking remedial action when the organization learns that a third party has
mishandled personal information shared by the organization

Security for Privacy

Protecting the security of personal information is deeply entwined with protecting the privacy of that information. Organizations can't provide individuals with assurances about the
handling of personal data if they can't protect that information from unauthorized access.
The PMF defines *security for privacy* as follows: "The entity protects PI against unauthorized
access, removal, alteration, destruction and disclosure (both physical and logical)."

The criteria associated with the security for privacy principle are as follows:

▶ Including security practices in the organization's privacy policies

▶ Informing individuals that the organization takes precautions to protect the
privacy of their personal information

▶ Developing, documenting, and implementing an information security
program that addresses the major privacy-related areas of security

▶ Restricting logical access to personal information through the use of strong
identification, authentication, and authorization practices

▶ Restricting physical access to personal information through the use of physical
security controls

▶ Protecting personal information from accidental disclosure due to natural
disasters and other environmental hazards

▶ Applying strong encryption to any personal information that is transmitted
over public networks

▶ Avoiding the storage of personal information on portable media, unless abso-
lutely necessary, and using encryption to protect any personal information
that must be stored on portable media

▶ Conducting periodic tests of security safeguards used to protect personal
information

Data Integrity and Quality

When we think about the issues associated with protecting the privacy of personal
information, we often first think about issues related to the proper collection and use of

that information along with potential unauthorized disclosure of that information. However, it's also important to consider the accuracy of that information. Individuals may be damaged by incorrect information just as much, if not more, than they might be damaged by information that is improperly handled. The PMF *data integrity and quality* principle states that "The entity maintains accurate, complete and relevant PI for the purposes identified in the notice and protects the representational integrity of the PI in its ongoing interactions with data subjects."

The criteria associated with the data integrity and quality principle are as follows:

▶ Including data quality practices in the organization's privacy policies
▶ Informing individuals that they bear responsibility for providing the organization with accurate and complete personal information and informing the organization if corrections are required
▶ Maintaining personal information that is accurate, complete, and relevant for the purposes for which it will be used

Monitoring and Enforcement

Privacy programs are not a onetime project. It's true that organizations may make a substantial initial investment of time and energy to build up their privacy practices, but those practices must be monitored over time to ensure that they continue to operate effectively and meet the organization's privacy obligations as business needs and information practices evolve. The PMF *monitoring and enforcement* principle states that "The entity monitors compliance with its privacy policies and procedures and has procedures to address privacy-related complaints and disputes."

The criteria associated with the monitoring and enforcement principle are as follows:

▶ Including monitoring and enforcement practices in the organization's privacy policies
▶ Informing individuals about how they should contact the organization if they have questions, complaints, or disputes regarding privacy practices
▶ Maintaining a dispute resolution process that ensures that every complaint is addressed and that the individual who raised the complaint is provided with a documented response
▶ Reviewing compliance with privacy policies, procedures, laws, regulations, and contractual obligations on an annual basis
▶ Developing and implementing remediation plans for any issues identified during privacy compliance reviews
▶ Documenting cases where privacy policies were violated and taking any necessary corrective action
▶ Performing ongoing monitoring of the privacy program based on a risk assessment

EXAM ESSENTIALS

▶ IT professionals have an obligation to protect the privacy of personal information, particularly when the individuals involved have a reasonable expectation of privacy.

▶ The types of personal information that must be safeguarded include personally identifiable information (PII), which is any personal information that may be tied to an individual, and protected health information (PHI), which includes medical records.

▶ The nine Privacy Management Framework (PMF) principles are as follows:

1. Management
2. Agreement, notice, and communication
3. Collection and creation
4. Use, retention, and disposal
5. Access
6. Disclosure to third parties
7. Security for privacy
8. Data integrity and quality
9. Monitoring and enforcement

Practice Question 1

Which of these people would have the least expectation of privacy?

A. A patient discussing medical records with a nurse
B. An employee sending an email to a friend over the office network
C. A student discussing grades with a teacher
D. Two people having a private conversation

Practice Question 2

Norm is reviewing his organization's privacy practices and observes that the privacy notice is not posted on their website in a location that is accessible to customers. Which PMF principle is most directly violated by this action?

A. Agreement, notice, and communication
B. Choice and consent
C. Communication
D. Collection and creation

Practice Question 1 Explanation

A patient discussing medical records with a nurse is in a situation where there is a strong expectation of privacy. These records are protected health information (PHI) and should be treated very carefully. Of the situations listed, this is likely the one with the greatest expectation of privacy.

A student discussing grades with a teacher and two people having a private conversation are also in situations where they should have some expectation of privacy.

An employee of an organization sending an email at work has no expectation of privacy. The employer is entitled to inspect any information sent or received using the office network, even if that information is of a personal nature.

Correct Answer: B. An employee sending an email to a friend in the office

Practice Question 2 Explanation

The second PMF principle—agreement, notice, and communication—requires that organizations inform individuals about their privacy practices. One of the criteria for this principle includes writing privacy notices in plain and simple language and posting them conspicuously. Norm's organization is not doing this.

This does not directly impact the principles of choice and consent or collection and creation.

Communication seems like an obvious answer here, but it is not one of the nine PMF principles.

Correct Answer: A. Agreement, notice, and communication

CHAPTER 4

Risk Management
Objective 1.2
Understand the Risk Management Process

Risks abound in the world of information security. From hackers and malware to lost devices and missing security patches, information security professionals have a lot on their plate. Of course, addressing each risk takes both time and money. Risk management is the practice of identifying, assessing, and treating the risks facing an organization.

In this chapter, you'll learn about CC objective 1.2. The following subobjectives are covered in this chapter:

▶ Risk management (e.g., risk priorities, risk tolerance)
▶ Risk identification, assessment, and treatment

RISK TYPES

The main responsibility of a cybersecurity professional is to manage risk. Organizations face many different kinds of risk, and it's your job to identify, assess, and manage those risks to protect your information and assets. This section discusses the different kinds of risk that exist in our everyday world.

Internal and External Risks

Risks can be divided into two categories: internal and external. *Internal risks* are those that arise from within the organization. For example, if the way that you process checks creates an opportunity for employees in the accounting department to commit fraud, then that's an example of an internal risk.

You can often address internal risks by adding *internal controls*. These security measures reduce the likelihood or impact of a risk occurring. In the accounting example, adding a two-person control to the issuance of checks might reduce the risk of fraud by requiring that two different people cooperate to issue a check.

External risks are those where the threat originates outside of the organization. For example, the risk of an attacker targeting your organization with a ransomware attack is external. You can't do much to stop the attacker from attempting the attack, but you can build controls that reduce the likelihood that the attack will be successful or its impact if it does occur, such as using multi-factor authentication or launching a social engineering threat awareness campaign.

Multiparty Risks

The next type of risk covered on the Certified in Cybersecurity (CC) exam is *multiparty risks*. These are risks that are shared among many different organizations. For example, if a software as a service (SaaS) provider is compromised, that is a multiparty risk because it poses a risk to all the customers of that service provider.

Specific Risks

In addition to the general categories of internal, external, and multiparty risks, there are a few specific risk types that you should be familiar with as you prepare for the CC exam. These are the risks associated with legacy systems, intellectual property, and software license compliance.

Legacy Systems

Legacy systems pose a unique type of risk to the organization. These systems have been around for a long time and remain in use despite their age and possible lack of maintenance. It's often difficult to secure older systems, especially those no longer supported by the manufacturer. Any organization using legacy systems should consider replacing them with a modern solution or carefully designing a set of security controls to mitigate the legacy risk.

Intellectual Property

In the information age, the value delivered by many businesses resides in their intellectual property. If attackers were able to alter, destroy, or steal this information, it would cause significant damage to the business. Therefore, intellectual property theft poses a risk to information-based organizations.

Software License Compliance

Finally, make sure that you consider the risks associated with software license compliance issues. Businesses often go to great lengths to protect their intellectual property investment in software, including performing audits of organizations and assessing significant fines to those who violate license agreements. It's a good idea to use license monitoring software to manage your software license compliance efforts.

RISK IDENTIFICATION AND ASSESSMENT

The world of cybersecurity is full of risks. As a result, you have to figure out how to allocate your limited time and resources to address the most important risks first. To accomplish this, you need to prioritize your risk lists so that you spend your precious resources where they will have the greatest security impact.

Risk identification and assessment is the process of identifying and triaging the risks facing an organization based on the likelihood of their occurrence and their expected impact on the organization.

The Language of Risk

First, we need a common language. In everyday life, people often use the terms *threat*, *vulnerability*, and *risk* interchangeably. However, they are actually three different concepts:

- ▶ *Threats* are external forces that jeopardize the security of your information and systems. Threats might be naturally occurring, such as hurricanes and wildfires, or human-made, such as hacking and terrorism. You can't normally control what threats are out there. They exist independently of you and your organization.
- ▶ *Vulnerabilities* are weaknesses in your security controls that a threat might exploit to undermine the confidentiality, integrity, or availability of your information or systems. These might include missing patches, promiscuous firewall rules, or other security misconfigurations. You *do* have control over the vulnerabilities in your environment, and security professionals spend much of their time hunting down and remediating vulnerabilities.
- ▶ *Risks* occur when your environment contains both a vulnerability and a corresponding threat that might exploit that vulnerability, as shown in Figure 4.1. For example, if you haven't patched a database server recently and hackers create malware that exploits an unpatched vulnerability, you face a risk. You are vulnerable because you're missing a security control and there is a threat: the new malware.

FIGURE 4.1   Risks are the combination of a threat and a corresponding vulnerability

There is no risk if either the threat or vulnerability factor is missing. For example, if you live in an area far from the coast, it doesn't matter if your building is vulnerable to hurricanes, because there is no threat of a hurricane in your region. Similarly, if you store your backup tapes in a fireproof box, there is a reduced risk of them being destroyed in a fire because your storage container is not vulnerable to fire.

> **EXAM TIP**
>
> There is one related term that you should know for the exam. A *threat vector* is the method that an attacker uses to get to a target. This might be a hacker toolkit, social engineering, or physical intrusion.

Ranking Risks

Once you've identified the risks facing your organization, you probably still have a some-what overwhelming list. The next stage in the process ranks those risks by two factors: likelihood and impact.

Risk Likelihood

The *likelihood* of a risk is the probability that it will actually occur. For example, there is a risk of earthquake in both California and Wisconsin. When you look at the data, however, you find that the probability of an earthquake occurring is far higher in California, where almost 5,000 significant earthquakes occurred over a 25-year period. During that same time, Wisconsin didn't experience a single major earthquake. Therefore, security profes-sionals in California must be hypervigilant about the risk of earthquakes, while those in Wisconsin can probably ignore it.

Risk Impact

The *impact* of a risk is the amount of damage that will occur if the risk materializes. For example, an earthquake might cause devastating damage to a data center, while a rain-storm might not cause any damage at all.

Risk Assessment Techniques

In risk assessments, two categories of techniques are available for assessing the likelihood and impact of a risk: qualitative techniques and quantitative techniques.

Qualitative techniques use subjective judgments to assess risks, typically categorizing them as low, medium, or high on both the likelihood and impact scales. Figure 4.2 shows an example of a qualitative risk assessment matrix. When considering a specific risk, the assessor first rates the likelihood as low, medium, or high, and then does the same for the impact. The chart then categorizes the overall risk. For example, a risk with a high likelihood and high impact would be categorized as a high risk, whereas a risk with a medium likelihood and low impact would be categorized overall as low.

Quantitative techniques use objective numeric ratings to assess the likelihood and impact of a risk. When performing a quantitative risk assessment, you'll do some mathematical cal-culations to determine the precise amount of financial damage you can expect from a given risk in any typical year.

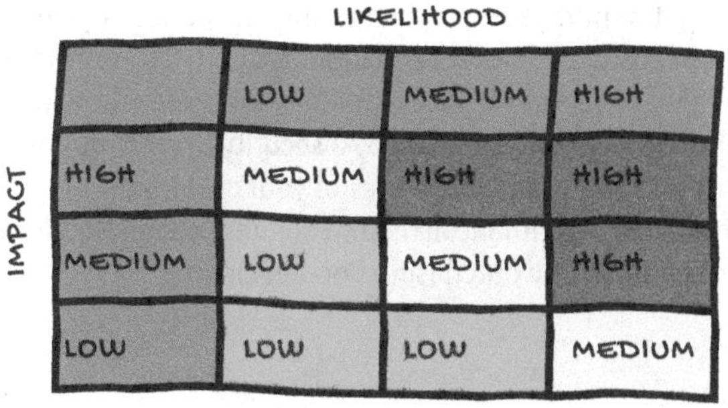

FIGURE 4.2 Qualitative risk assessment

EXAM TIP

You don't need to know how to do the math for a quantitative risk assessment on the CC exam, but you'll learn it if you move on to prepare for the CISSP or other advanced cybersecurity certifications.

RISK TREATMENT STRATEGIES

Once you complete a risk assessment for your organization, you're left with a prioritized list of risks that require your attention. *Risk treatment* is the process of systematically analyzing potential responses to each risk and implementing strategies to control those risks appropriately.

No matter which risk you're managing, you have four basic options for addressing the situation. You can:

▶ Avoid the risk
▶ Transfer the risk
▶ Mitigate the risk
▶ Accept the risk

Risk Avoidance

When you practice *risk avoidance*, you change your organization's business practices so that you are no longer in a position where that risk can affect your business.

For example, imagine that you performed a risk assessment of the risk that flooding posed to your organization's data center. If you chose to pursue a risk avoidance strategy for that risk, you might relocate your data center to a facility where there is no risk of flood damage.

Risk Transference

Risk transference attempts to shift the impact of a risk from your organization to another organization. The most common example of risk transference is an insurance policy.

Many organizations are now considering the purchase of cybersecurity insurance policies to protect against the financial damage caused by hackers and identity theft. It's important to remember, however, that you can't always transfer a risk completely. For example, you can purchase insurance to cover the financial damage caused by a security breach, but no insurance policy can repair your business's reputation in the eyes of your customers.

In the flood risk example, you might transfer the financial risk of your data center flooding from your organization to an insurance company by purchasing flood insurance.

Risk Mitigation

Risk mitigation takes actions designed to reduce the likelihood and/or impact of a risk.

If you want to mitigate the risk of your data center flooding, you might engage a flood control specialist to install systems designed to divert water away from your facility.

Risk Acceptance

In almost every risk assessment, managers find themselves confronted with a very long list of risks and inadequate resources to avoid, transfer, or mitigate all of them. For business reasons, they must accept some of those risks.

Risk acceptance should only take place as part of a thoughtful analysis that determines that the cost of performing another risk management action outweighs the benefit of controlling the risk.

In the flooding scenario, you might conclude that all of the other risk management options are too costly and decide to continue operations in your current facility as is and deal with the aftermath of a flood should it occur.

RISK PROFILE AND TOLERANCE

Every organization must choose the appropriate mix of risk treatment strategies for their own technical and business environment. The combination of risks that affect an organization are known as its *risk profile*, and the organization adopts risk treatment strategies to address the risks in that profile.

Figure 4.3 shows the process that an organization goes through as it manages risk. The initial level of risk that exists in an organization before any controls are put in place is the organization's *inherent risk*. Then controls are applied to reduce that risk, but, of course, not every risk can be completely eliminated. The risk that remains after the inherent risk is reduced by controls is known as the *residual risk*.

Controls themselves may introduce some new risk. For example, if you install a firewall as a risk management control, that may reduce your risk substantially, but it also adds a new risk that the firewall itself may fail. That new risk that results from adding controls is known as *control risk*.

The reality is that the organization will need to accept some ongoing risk in order to continue operations. Business leaders must decide how much risk they choose to accept. This is a process known as determining the organization's *risk tolerance*.

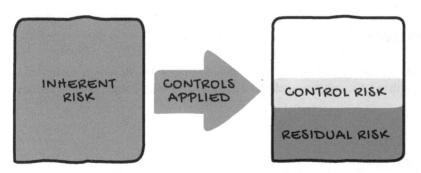

FIGURE 4.3 Applying controls reduces the inherent risk down to the residual risk but also introduces control risk.

EXAM TIP

The goal of risk management is to make sure that the combination of the residual risk and the control risk is below the organization's risk tolerance.

EXAM ESSENTIALS

▶ Internal risks are those that arise from within the organization. External risks are those where the threat originates outside of the organization. Multiparty risks are shared among many different organizations.

▶ Threats are external forces that jeopardize the security of your information and systems. Vulnerabilities are weaknesses in your security controls that a threat might exploit to undermine the confidentiality, integrity, or availability of your information or systems. Risks occur when your environment contains both a vulnerability and a corresponding threat that might exploit that vulnerability.

▶ Risks are prioritized based on their likelihood and impact. The likelihood of a risk is the probability that it will actually occur. The impact of a risk is the amount of damage that will occur if the risk materializes.

▶ Qualitative risk assessment techniques use subjective judgments to assess risks, typically categorizing them as low, medium, or high on both the likelihood and impact scales. Quantitative risk assessment techniques use objective numeric ratings to assess the likelihood and impact of a risk.

▶ The four risk treatment options are avoiding a risk, transferring a risk, mitigating a risk, and accepting a risk.

▶ An organization's risk profile begins with its inherent risk. Security professionals then apply controls to reduce that inherent risk, leaving the remaining residual risk. Controls may introduce new control risks.

Practice Question 1

Jen identified a missing patch on a Windows server that might allow an attacker to gain remote control of the system. After consulting with her manager, she applied the patch. From a risk management perspective, what has she done?

A. Removed the threat
B. Reduced the threat
C. Removed the vulnerability
D. Reduced the vulnerability

Practice Question 2

Grace recently completed a risk assessment of her organization's exposure to data breaches and determined that there is a high level of risk related to the loss of sensitive personal information due to a type of attack called SQL injection. She is considering a variety of approaches to managing this risk.

Grace's first idea is to add a web application firewall to protect her organization against SQL injection attacks. Which risk management strategy does this approach adopt?

A. Risk acceptance
B. Risk avoidance
C. Risk mitigation
D. Risk transference

Practice Question 1 Explanation

Jen can reduce the risk associated with the missing patch by taking one of two courses of action. She can either reduce/remove the threat or reduce/remove the vulnerability.

Jen has no control over what an external attacker does, so she is unable to reduce or remove the threat.

However, she does have control over the patch status of the system. By applying the patch, Jen has removed the vulnerability from her server. This goes beyond actions that would simply reduce the vulnerability, such as adding an additional firewall.

Correct Answer: C. Removed the vulnerability

Practice Question 2 Explanation

Installing new controls or upgrading existing controls is an effort to reduce the likelihood or impact of a risk. This is an example of a risk mitigation activity because risk mitigation activities are designed to reduce the likelihood or impact of a risk.

If Grace were to take a risk acceptance strategy, she would simply acknowledge that her organization was vulnerable to SQL injection attacks and take no further action.

If Grace wanted to pursue risk avoidance, she would shut down any systems that might be vulnerable to SQL injection attacks.

If Grace wanted to pursue risk transference, she would transfer the potential financial burden of the risk to a third party, such as by purchasing an insurance policy.

Correct Answer: C. Risk mitigation

CHAPTER 5

Security Controls
Objective 1.3 Understand Security Controls

Security professionals spend the majority of their time designing, implementing, and managing security controls as countermeasures to the risks they identify during risk assessments. It's important that security professionals have a strong understanding of the different types of controls and how they work.

In this chapter, you'll learn about CC objective 1.3. The following subobjectives are covered in this chapter:

▶ **Technical controls**
▶ **Administrative controls**
▶ **Physical controls**

WHAT ARE SECURITY CONTROLS?

Security controls are procedures and mechanisms that an organization puts in place to address security risks in some manner. This might include trying to reduce the likelihood of a risk materializing, minimize the impact of the risk if it does occur, or detect security issues that do occur.

Before moving into the area of cybersecurity, consider for a moment the way that you secure your home. You probably use a variety of different security controls. Some of them might include the following:

▶ Locks on your doors and windows designed to keep out intruders
▶ A burglar alarm designed to detect intrusions
▶ Security cameras to record activity inside and outside your home
▶ Automatic light switches to deter a burglar by simulating human activity

Some of these controls are designed to achieve the same purpose or, in the language of security professionals, the same *control objective*. For example, both a burglar alarm and security cameras are designed to detect intruders. We sometimes use more than one control to achieve the same objective because we want to be sure that we remain secure even if one control fails. If a burglar manages to open a window without tripping the burglar alarm, they may still be caught on your security cameras. This is known as the *defense in depth principle*—applying multiple overlapping controls to achieve the same objective.

CATEGORIZING SECURITY CONTROLS

Security professionals use a variety of different categories to group similar security controls. I'll talk about two different ways. First, I'll discuss grouping controls by their purpose—whether they are designed to prevent, detect, or recover from security issues. Then, I'll discuss them by their mechanism of action—the way they work. This groups them into the categories of technical, administrative, and physical controls.

Purpose Categories

When security controls are categorized by their purpose, they are grouped into categories by their intent—that is, whether they are designed to prevent, detect, or recover from security incidents.

Preventive controls are designed to stop a security issue from occurring in the first place. A firewall that blocks unwanted network traffic is an example of a preventive control.

Detective controls identify potential security breaches that require further investigation. An intrusion detection system that searches for signs of network breaches is an example of a detective control.

Recovery controls remediate security issues that have already occurred. If ransomware infects a system and wipes out critical information, restoring that information from backup is an example of a recovery control.

Let's dig into that ransomware example a little more and talk about the ways that different controls can help protect you against ransomware. As you may know, ransomware infects systems and uses encryption to prevent users from accessing files until they pay a ransom. Consider the following three different controls that can be put in place to protect against ransomware:

- ▶ You might perform system hardening. That locks down the security of your system to protect it from experiencing an attack in the first place. System hardening prevents ransomware infections, so it is a preventive control.
- ▶ You might run regular antivirus scans to detect ransomware on your system. Those scans will alert you to the presence of an infection, so they are a detective control.
- ▶ If you do get a ransomware infection, those preventive and detective controls aren't going to help you get your data back. That's where you need your backups—a recovery control.

Mechanism of Action Categories

The second way to categorize controls is by their mechanism of action. This groups controls as either technical, administrative, or physical controls.

Technical controls are exactly what the name implies, the use of technology to achieve security objectives. Think about all of the components of an IT infrastructure that perform security functions. Firewalls, intrusion prevention systems, encryption, data loss prevention, and antivirus software are all examples of technical security controls.

> **EXAM TIP**
>
> If you see someone use the term *logical controls*, that's the same thing as *technical controls*. *Logical* and *technical* are two different words that describe the same type of control.

Administrative controls include the processes that you put in place to manage technology in a secure manner. These include many of the tasks that security professionals carry out each day, such as user access reviews, log monitoring, background checks, and security awareness training.

Physical controls are those that impact the physical world. Locks are used to keep people out of buildings, cameras to detect unauthorized intrusions, and security guards to monitor activity in our facilities. All of these are examples of physical controls.

As you work to design security for your organization, you'll want to use a variety of different control types to help achieve your security objectives.

EXAM ESSENTIALS

▶ **Security controls can be classified by their purpose and by their mechanism of action.**

▶ **The purpose categories are preventive, detective, and recovery.** Preventive controls are designed to stop a security issue from occurring in the first place. Detective controls identify potential security breaches that require further investigation. Recovery controls remediate security issues that have already occurred. If ransomware infects a system and wipes out critical information, restoring that information from backup is an example of a recovery control.

▶ **The mechanism of action categories are technical, administrative, and physical.** Technical controls use technology to achieve security objectives. Administrative controls are the processes that you put in place to manage technology in a secure manner. Physical controls are those that impact the physical world.

Practice Question 1

Tonya is concerned about the risk that an attacker will attempt to gain access to her organization's database server. She is searching for a control that would block the attacker's attempts to gain access. Which type of security control is she seeking to implement?

A. Technical
B. Detective
C. Recovery
D. Preventive

Practice Question 2

Tonya evaluated all of the options available to her for protecting her database and decided to implement strong encryption to protect the contents of the data in her database. Which mechanism of action is she using?

A. Technical
B. Administrative
C. Preventive
D. Physical

Practice Question 1 Explanation

Tonya is attempting to stop the attacker from gaining access to a system in the first place, so this is an example of a preventive control. She hopes to prevent a security incident from occurring.

Recovery controls are used to remediate security issues that have already occurred. If an attacker did compromise a system and Tonya rebuilt that system to remove the damage, that would be a recovery control.

Detective controls identify potential security breaches. If Tonya installed an intrusion detection system that alerted her to compromised systems, that would be an example of a detective control.

It is possible that Tonya may deploy a technical control, but all we know from this scenario is the *purpose* of the desired control: to prevent compromises. There is no preference described for the mechanism of action for that preventive control.

Correct Answer: D. Preventive

Practice Question 2 Explanation

Technical controls use technology to achieve security objectives. In this scenario, Tonya is using encryption technology to protect the contents of her database, so she is implementing a technical control.

Administrative controls are the processes that are put in place to manage technology in a secure manner. There is no discussion of processes in this scenario, so Tonya is not implementing an administrative control.

Physical controls are those that impact the physical world. Encryption is a digital technology and does not impact the physical world, so it is not a physical control.

This use of encryption is a preventive control, but preventive is a purpose category, not a mechanism of action category. The question specifically asked for the mechanism of action.

Correct Answer: A. Technical

CHAPTER 6

Ethics
Objective 1.4 Understand ISC2 Code of Ethics

Ethics guide the way that we behave and handle our personal and professional responsibilities. While each of us has our own internal sense of ethics, we also are subject to ethical codes provided by others. Many employers have written ethical standards that apply to all employees. The International Information System Security Certification Consortium ISC2 has a Code of Ethics that applies to the behavior of all ISC2 members.

In this chapter, you'll learn about CC objective 1.4. The following subobjective is covered in this chapter:

▶ **Professional code of conduct**

CORPORATE ETHICS CODES

Codes of professional ethics require that information security professionals act honorably and responsibly. Because information security professionals are often entrusted with highly sensitive data, it is critical that they act in a way that is ethical and trustworthy.

Many organizations have internal codes of ethics that their employees must follow. These codes outline the principles and guidelines that employees are expected to follow to ensure that they act honestly and ethically, and that they avoid personal conflicts of interest.

For example, Figure 6.1 shows a portion of the Code of Business Conduct for AT&T. It includes rules and guidelines for how employees should conduct themselves honestly and ethically and avoid personal conflicts of interest.

AT&T's code is quite typical of those used by large organizations. If you'd like to review this multipage document in detail, you can find it at `https://cobc.att.com/mission`.

Our Commitment to Honesty and to Each Other

We are honest and act with integrity.

This statement applies to everything we do at AT&T. Our daily interactions should start and end with honesty and integrity. We hold ourselves and each other to a high standard of ethical behavior. Many groups - shareholders, customers, communities, suppliers, public authorities, our fellow employees - are able to trust what we say and do. We take personal responsibility for meeting the goals we share and keeping our commitments.

We treat each other with respect and do not permit intimidation, discrimination or harassment in the workplace.

When the actions of some cause others to feel intimidated, offended or to lose dignity, all of us suffer. We must treat each other courteously and professionally. We insist on a positive work environment, and speak out if that goal is compromised by anyone.

FIGURE 6.1 AT&T's Code of Business Conduct

By adhering to these codes of ethics, information security professionals can build trust with their colleagues and clients, and protect themselves from legal and ethical repercussions. These codes help to promote a culture of transparency, accountability, and responsibility within organizations, which ultimately benefits everyone involved.

ISC2 CODE OF ETHICS

ISC2 also has a code of ethics that applies to all certified security professionals. The *ISC2 Code of Ethics* includes four canons—four simple statements that outline what is expected of individuals who subscribe to the code:

1. Protect society, the common good, necessary public trust and confidence, and the infrastructure.
2. Act honorably, honestly, justly, responsibly, and legally.
3. Provide diligent and competent service to principals.
4. Advance and protect the profession.

You'll want to be very familiar with these canons when you take the exam. You don't necessarily need to be able to recite them word-for-word, but you do need to know the general idea behind each one.

Canon 1

The first canon of the code of ethics is that you must protect society, its infrastructure, and the common good. The actions you take should give the public confidence in our profession. This canon basically means that the actions you take, or fail to take, must support the betterment of society. As a certified security professional, you have an obligation to protect the common good. For example, a security professional who uses their skills to engage in unethical hacking activities would violate this canon of the code.

Canon 2

The second canon is that your actions must be ethical. You must act with honor, justice, and responsibility and work within the bounds of the law. The bottom line here is that you may not break the law, lie, or commit any other dishonorable, unjust, or irresponsible action. For example, a security professional who makes an error that leads to a compromise at their organization and then covers up and lies about the mistake is violating this canon of the code of ethics.

Canon 3

The third canon is that the professional services you provide to principals must be both diligent and competent. As a security professional, you must carry out your duties in a responsible manner. The code uses the word *principal* here because it is meant to apply to your employer if you are a normal employee or to your clients if you are a consultant. Basically, whomever you are working for has the right to expect your diligent and competent service. A security professional who fails to carry out their assigned and agreed-upon duties is violating this canon.

Canon 4

Finally, the fourth canon is that your actions as a security professional should advance and protect the information security profession. The actions you take should help, rather than detract from, the profession at large. The most common way that this canon is violated is when certified individuals provide unauthorized assistance on exams, violate the ISC2 nondisclosure agreement, or provide false information on an applicant's endorsement application.

> **EXAM TIP**
> When you take the CC exam, you should not only remember the main idea behind each of the four canons, but you should also be able to analyze an ethical issue and identify the canon(s) that might have been violated.

ETHICS COMPLAINT PROCEDURE

You must follow a formal process if you suspect that another ISC2 member has violated the ISC2 Code of Ethics. The code does contain a statement requiring you to report violations of the code. In fact, failure to report a violation that you know of is itself a violation of the code of ethics. So, if you witness a violation of the code of ethics and do not report it, you yourself are violating the code and are subject to sanctions.

If you are in a situation where you need to submit a violation report, you must submit a written, notarized affidavit using the form supplied on the ISC2 website. It must include the name of the accused person, the nature of the violation, the specific canon or canons breached, the reason you have standing, and any corroborating evidence.

Having *standing* to file a complaint means that the alleged behavior must harm you or your profession in some way. Standing varies based on the canon involved.

> ▶ Canons 1 and 2 are about protecting society at large and acting responsibly. Anyone may be harmed by those violations, so any member of the public has standing to file a complaint about Canons 1 and 2.
> ▶ Canon 3 is about service to principals (employers or clients), so only employers or clients of the individual have standing to file a complaint about Canon 3.
> ▶ Canon 4 is about protecting the profession, so other professionals have standing to file a complaint about Canon 4 violations. This doesn't mean that you have to be ISC2 certified or even a security professional. Anyone who is certified or licensed in any field and subscribes to a code of ethics may file a Canon 4 complaint. For example, a certified public accountant or a licensed health care professional would have standing to file a Canon 4 complaint.

Once a complaint is filed, the ISC2 Ethics Committee takes over. They will allow the accused individual to respond, gather any additional evidence that they wish, and reach a determination. If they find an individual has violated the Code of Ethics, they may revoke that individual's certification.

EXAM TIP

It's really important that you understand who can file a complaint under each canon. You should be able to read a scenario, recognize which canons might have been violated, and describe who has standing to file a complaint under that canon.

EXAM ESSENTIALS

▶ Canon 1 of the ISC2 Code of Ethics says that you must protect society, the common good, necessary public trust and confidence, and the infrastructure. Anyone may file a complaint against a member under Canon 1.

▶ Canon 2 of the ISC2 Code of Ethics says that you must act honorably, honestly, justly, responsibly, and legally. Anyone may file a complaint against a member under Canon 2.

▶ Canon 3 of the ISC2 Code of Ethics says that you must provide diligent and competent service to principals. Only one of those principals (an individual's employer or consulting client) may file a complaint against a member under Canon 3.

▶ Canon 4 of the ISC2 Code of Ethics says that you must advance and protect the profession. Any certified professional who subscribes to an ethical code may file a complaint against a member under Canon 4.

Practice Question 1

You are the supervisor of a team of cybersecurity professionals, all of whom hold current ISC2 certifications. You believe that one of those employees has stolen funds from your organization, and an internal investigation confirmed the likelihood of that action. Which two canons of the Code of Ethics were most likely violated?

A. Canons 1 and 2
B. Canons 2 and 3
C. Canons 3 and 4
D. Canons 1 and 4

Practice Question 2

You have witnessed behavior by a certified cybersecurity professional and ISC2 member that you believe directly harms the cybersecurity profession. Who has standing to file a complaint about this behavior?

A. Any member of the public
B. Any certified professional
C. The individual's employer or consulting client
D. Nobody

Practice Question 1 Explanation

Canon 1 is that you must protect society, the common good, necessary public trust and confidence, and the infrastructure. Although stealing from an employer is certainly not ethical behavior, it doesn't likely rise to the level of harming society that is described by this question.

Canon 2 is that you must act honorably, honestly, justly, responsibly, and legally. In this case, the employee who stole certainly did not act in accordance with these principles. Based on this information alone, you can select the answer "Canons 2 and 3" because it is the only one that includes Canon 2—but let's continue the analysis just to confirm.

Canon 3 is that you must provide diligent and competent service to principals (such as your employer). Stealing from your employer is certainly not competent service, so there is a good argument that Canon 3 was violated.

Canon 4 is that you must advance and protect the profession. As with the Canon 1 analysis, the employee's behavior was certainly not ethical, but it doesn't really rise to the level of harming the profession.

Correct Answer: B. Canons 2 and 3

Practice Question 2 Explanation

To answer this question, you must first identify which canon of the ISC2 Code of Ethics is involved. Canon 4 of the code is to "Advance and protect the profession," which seems to match the scenario provided here.

Next, you must know who has standing to file a complaint under that particular canon. According to the complaint procedures, any certified professional may file a complaint under Canon 4.

Any member of the public is entitled to file an ethics complaint under Canons 1 and 2, but not under Canon 4.

An individual's employer or consulting client may file an ethics complaint under Canon 3, but not under Canon 4.

Correct Answer: B. Any certified professional

CHAPTER 7

Security Governance Processes

Objective 1.5 Understand Governance Processes

Security governance processes are an integral part of safeguarding an organization's data and infrastructure. Policies, procedures, standards, and laws all play an important role in directing the actions of cybersecurity professionals and other team members.

In this chapter, you'll learn about CC objective 1.5. The following subobjectives are covered in this chapter:

▶ **Policies**
▶ **Procedures**
▶ **Standards**
▶ **Regulations and laws**

SECURITY POLICIES AND PROCEDURES

Security professionals do a lot of writing! We need clearly written guidance to help communicate to business leaders, end users, and each other about security obligations, expectations, and responsibilities. In some cases, we're setting forth mandatory rules that everyone in the organization must follow; in other cases, we're simply giving advice. Each of these roles requires communicating a bit differently.

That's where the security policy framework comes into play. Most security professionals recognize a framework consisting of four different types of documents: policies, standards, guidelines, and procedures.

Security Policies

Security policies are the bedrock documents that provide the foundation for an organization's information security program. They are often developed over a long period of time and carefully written to describe an organization's security expectations.

Compliance with policies is mandatory, and policies are often approved at the very highest levels of an organization. Because of the rigor involved in developing security policies, authors should strive to write them in a way that will stand the test of time.

For example, statements like "All sensitive information must be encrypted with AES-256 encryption" or "Store all employee records in Room 225" are not good policy statements. What happens if the organization switches encryption technologies or moves its records room?

Instead, a policy might make statements like "Sensitive information must be encrypted both at rest and in transit using technology approved by the IT department" and "Employee records must be stored in a location approved by Human Resources." Those statements are much more likely to stand the test of time.

Security Standards

Security standards prescribe the specific details of security controls that the organization must follow. Standards derive their authority from policy. In fact, it's likely that an organization's security policy would include specific statements giving the IT department authority to create and enforce standards. They're the place to include things like the company's approved encryption protocols, record storage locations, configuration parameters, and other technical and operational details.

Even though standards might not go through as rigorous a process as policies, compliance with them is still mandatory.

Security Guidelines

Security professionals use *guidelines* to provide advice to the rest of the organization, including best practices for information security. For example, a guideline might suggest that employees use encrypted wireless networks whenever they are available. There might be situations where a traveling employee does not have access to an encrypted network, so they can compensate for that by using a VPN connection. Remember, guidelines are advice. Compliance with guidelines is not mandatory.

Security Procedures

Procedures are step-by-step instructions that employees must follow when performing a specific security task. For example, the organization might have a procedure for activating the incident response team that involves sending an urgent SMS alert to team members, activating a videoconference, and informing senior management.

Compliance with procedures is mandatory.

> **EXAM TIP**
> When taking the CC exam, be sure that you keep the differences between policies, standards, guidelines, and procedures straight. Specifically, remember that compliance with policies, standards, and procedures is always mandatory. Complying with guidelines is optional.

LAWS AND REGULATIONS

Whenever we work with sensitive information, we encounter laws and regulations that govern how we store, process, and transmit that information. One of the first things that we need to figure out when working with sensitive data is what specific laws and regulations apply to us. While that might sound straightforward at first glance, the question of which jurisdictions have authority to regulate data is actually quite complicated, and compliance risks can impact an organization's risk posture.

Consider a simple example. Imagine a company with all of its operations located in the state of California. It's clear in this case that California state and local laws and regulations apply to the company, and so does federal law written at the national level in the United States. But what if the company has a customer located in New York? Does New York law now apply as well? And if the company is using a cloud provider located in Texas, does Texas law govern the data? If that cloud provider outsources to a data center provider in Florida, then what?

The issue becomes even more complicated when expanded internationally. The European Union says that their *General Data Protection Regulation (GDPR)* applies to the personal information of all EU residents, wherever they might be located. Of course, GDPR isn't the only regulation that you'll need to follow. For example, health care providers in the United States must comply with the Health Insurance Portability and Accountability Act (HIPAA), while financial institutions must comply with the Gramm-Leach-Bliley Act (GLBA). Security professionals should be aware of the different national, territory, state, and local laws and regulations that apply to their operations.

Some regulations come from sources other than the law. For example, the *Payment Card Industry Data Security Standard (PCI DSS)* is a self-regulatory program that applies to credit and debit card transactions worldwide. Compliance is enforced by the banks that provide access to the payment card system.

There's no easy answer to these jurisdictional questions. You'll need to sort through these sometimes conflicting regulations with the help of your attorneys and develop a path that helps you evaluate legal risks that are appropriate for your operating environment.

EXAM ESSENTIALS

▶ The common types of security documents include policies, standards, guidelines, and procedures. Compliance with policies, standards, and procedures is always mandatory.

▶ Security professionals must be aware of all the laws and regulations that apply to them across the jurisdictions where their organizations operate. These may include national, state, and local laws. The European Union's General Data Protection Regulation (GDPR) applies to the personal information of EU residents.

▶ Some industries are also governed by self-regulatory frameworks. The most common example of these is the Payment Card Industry Data Security Standard (PCI DSS), which regulates the storage, processing, and transmission of credit and debit card information.

Practice Question 1

Your organization is planning to accept credit cards for the first time and you are concerned about the regulations that may affect this processing. You already handle a large amount of personally identifiable information (PII). Which new regulation is most likely to affect your organization?

A. GDPR
B. PCI DSS
C. CCPA
D. HIPAA

Practice Question 2

You are writing a document that explains the step-by-step process that your organization's help desk should follow when helping a user reset a forgotten password. Which type of document are you creating?

A. Policy
B. Standard
C. Procedure
D. Guideline

Practice Question 1 Explanation

The Payment Card Industry Data Security Standard (PCI DSS), which regulates the storage, processing, and transmission of credit and debit card information, would most likely apply in this scenario.

The European Union's General Data Protection Regulation (GDPR) and the California Consumer Privacy Act (CCPA) may also apply to this information, depending on where the organization operates. However, this would not be a new law because the organization already processes other PII, and both GDPR and CCPA would apply if the company operates in the European Union and/or California.

The Health Insurance Portability and Accountability Act (HIPAA) governs protected health information (PHI). There is no indication in this question that any health records are involved.

Correct Answer: B. PCI DSS

Practice Question 2 Explanation

The key to answering this question correctly is noticing that the document is a step-by-step process. This type of process should be documented in a procedure.

Security policies are high-level documents that would not contain technical details and certainly would not include the specific steps followed by a help desk. Standards normally describe technical requirements for information and systems. Guidelines are optional processes that provide best practice advice.

Correct Answer: C. Procedure

Domain 2: Business Continuity (BC), Disaster Recovery (DR) & Incident Response (IR) Concepts

Business Continuity (BC), Disaster Recovery (DR) & Incident Response (IR) Concepts is the second domain of ISC2's Certified in Cybersecurity exam. It provides the information that cybersecurity professionals need to know to protect the availability of information and systems and respond to security incidents. This domain includes the following three objectives:

2.1   **Understand business continuity (BC)**
2.2   **Understand disaster recovery (DR)**
2.3   **Understand incident response (IR)**

Questions from this domain make up 10 percent of the questions on the CC exam, so you should expect to see 10 questions on your test covering the material in this part.

CHAPTER 8

Business Continuity
Objective 2.1 Understand Business Continuity (BC)

Cybersecurity professionals are responsible for maintaining the availability of systems and data as one of their key functions. They must ensure that authorized individuals have access to the resources they need as part of a service provision or to get their work done. Business continuity comprises the core activities that assist in meeting this goal.

In this chapter, you'll learn about CC objective 2.1. The following subobjectives are covered in this chapter:

▶ **Purpose**
▶ **Importance**
▶ **Components**

BUSINESS CONTINUITY PLANNING

Business continuity planning (BCP) is one of the core responsibilities of the information security profession. *Business continuity* efforts are activities designed to keep a business running in the face of adversity. This may come in the form of a small-scale incident, such as a single system failure, or a catastrophic incident, such as an earthquake or tornado. Business continuity plans may also be activated by hazards caused by humans, such as a terrorist attack or hacker intrusion.

The focus of business continuity is keeping operations running, so BCP is sometimes referred to as continuity of operations planning (COOP).

While many organizations place the responsibility for business continuity with operational engineering teams, business continuity is a core security concept because it is the primary control that supports the security objective of availability. Remember, that's one of the "big three" objectives of information security: confidentiality, integrity, and availability.

BCP Scope Definition

When an organization begins a business continuity effort, it's easy to quickly become overwhelmed by the many possible scenarios and controls that the project might consider. For this reason, the team developing a business continuity plan should take time up front to carefully define their scope. Here are three questions that can help define the scope:

▶ Which business activities will the plan cover?
▶ What types of systems will the plan cover?
▶ What types of controls will the plan consider?

The answers to these questions will help you make critical prioritization decisions in later stages.

Business Impact Analysis

Continuity planners use a process known as a *business impact analysis (BIA)* to help make scope decisions. The BIA is an impact assessment that begins by identifying the organization's mission-essential functions and then traces those backward to identify the critical IT systems that support those processes. Once planners have identified the affected IT systems, they identify the potential risks, likelihood, and impacts to those systems as part of a risk assessment.

The output of a business impact analysis is a prioritized listing of risks and potential impacts that might disrupt the organization's business, such as the one shown in Table 8.1. Planners can then use this information to help select controls that mitigate the risks facing the organization within acceptable expense limits. For example, notice that the risks in this scenario are listed in descending order of expected loss.

TABLE 8.1 **Example of prioritized risks and potential impacts**

Risk	Annualized Loss Expectancy
Hurricane damage to the data center	$145,000
Fire in data center	$18,000
Power outage	$12,000
Theft of equipment	$3,400

It makes sense to prioritize the highest-risk item at the top of the list (hurricane damage to the data center). However, the organization must also consider cost when making decisions about control implementation. For example, if a $50,000 flood prevention system would reduce the risk of hurricane damage to the data center by 50 percent, purchasing the system is clearly a good decision because it has an expected payback period of less than one year.

In a cloud-centric environment, BCP becomes a collaboration between the cloud service provider (CSP) and the customer. For example, the risk of a hurricane damaging a data center may be mitigated by the service provider building a flood prevention system, but it also may be mitigated by the customer choosing to replicate services across data centers, availability zones, and geographic regions.

BUSINESS CONTINUITY CONTROLS

Business continuity professionals have a variety of tools at their disposal to help remediate potential availability issues. One of the critical ways that IT professionals protect the availability of systems is ensuring that they are redundant and fault-tolerant. That simply means that they are designed in such a way that the failure of a single component doesn't bring down the entire system—business can continue in the face of a single predictable component failure.

Single Point of Failure Analysis

The single point of failure (SPOF) analysis process provides security professionals with a mechanism to identify and remove single points of failure from their systems or processes.

Consider a simple example. Figure 8.1 shows a simple web-based application: a web server protected by a firewall and connected to the Internet.

WEB SERVER   FIREWALL   INTERNET

FIGURE 8.1 Web-based application

When conducting a single point of failure analysis, you might first notice that the web server itself is a single point of failure. If anything goes wrong with the server, the web service will stop functioning. You can correct this situation by replacing the single web server with a clustered farm of servers that are all designed to provide web services, as shown in Figure 8.2.

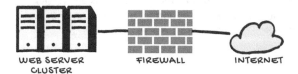

WEB SERVER   FIREWALL   INTERNET
CLUSTER

FIGURE 8.2 Adding clustered web servers

The cluster is designed so that if a single server fails, the other servers will continue providing service without disruption. Once you've implemented the cluster, you've removed the server as a single point of failure. Next, you might turn your attention to the firewall, another single point of failure. If the firewall goes down, Internet users will not be able to reach the web server, rendering the web service unavailable. Therefore, the firewall is also a single point of failure.

You can correct this situation by replacing the firewall with a pair of high availability firewalls, as shown in Figure 8.3.

WEB SERVER CLUSTER   HIGH AVAILABILITY FIREWALLS   INTERNET

FIGURE 8.3 Adding high availability firewalls

In this approach, one firewall serves as a backup device, standing by to step in immediately if the primary firewall fails. By replacing the single firewall with a high availability pair, you've removed the firewall as a single point of failure.

There are two other single points of failure here: the internal and external network connections. As with the web server and firewall, you can address this single point of failure by introducing redundancy, as shown in Figure 8.4. In this approach, each link has two separate network connections. If one fails, the service will continue to operate over the other.

WEB SERVER CLUSTER   HIGH AVAILABILITY FIREWALLS   INTERNET

FIGURE 8.4 Adding redundant network links

This single point of failure analysis may continue on, identifying and remediating issues until either the team stops finding new issues or the cost of addressing issues outweighs the potential benefit. Single point of failure analysis is an important part of an organization's continuity of operations planning efforts.

Other Continuity Risks

Organizations should also consider the other risks facing their IT operations. As they conduct IT contingency planning, they should consider not only single points of failure but also all of the other situations that might jeopardize business continuity. For example, these might include:

- ▶ Sudden bankruptcy of a key vendor
- ▶ Inability to provide the requisite computing or storage capacity
- ▶ Utility service failures
- ▶ Any other risk that IT management believes may disrupt operations

One final component of business continuity planning often overlooked is personnel succession planning. Information technology depends on highly skilled team members who develop, configure, and maintain systems and processes. IT leadership should work with their human resources department to identify team members essential to continued operations and identify potential successors to those positions. That way, when someone leaves the organization, management has already thought through potential replacements and, hopefully, provided those successors with the professional development opportunities they need to step into the departing employee's shoes.

HIGH AVAILABILITY AND FAULT TOLERANCE

I've already discussed some of the ways that security professionals can ensure the continued operation of systems. This section digs into this in a little more detail. There are two key technical concepts that improve the availability of systems: high availability and fault tolerance.

High Availability

High availability (HA) uses multiple systems to protect against failures. These are techniques like those discussed in the previous section. One example is to have a cluster of web servers in place that can continue to operate even if a single server fails. Another example is to use a pair of firewalls, with one designated as the backup. The core concept of high availability is having operationally redundant systems, sometimes at different sites. The geographic dispersal of placing systems in different locations protects you against damage to a facility.

LOAD BALANCING

Load balancing is a related but different concept from high availability. Load balancing uses multiple systems to spread out the burden of providing service across those systems, providing a scalable computing environment. While they use similar technologies, load balancing and high availability are different goals. Most implementations of clustering and similar technologies are designed to achieve both high availability and load balancing, but it is possible to have one without the other.

Fault Tolerance

Fault tolerance (FT) helps to protect a single system from failing in the first place by making it resilient in the face of technical failures. Three of the most common points of failure within a computer system are the device's:

▶ Power supply
▶ Storage media
▶ Networking components

Fault tolerance controls can prevent the system from failing even if one of these components fails completely.

Power Supplies

Power supplies contain moving parts and therefore are common points of failure. If a power supply fails, the results can be catastrophic. For this reason, server manufacturers often build dual power supplies into their servers, as shown in Figure 8.5.

FIGURE 8.5 Server with dual power supplies
Source: SasaStock/Adobe Stock

When a customer installs the server, they connect both of the power supplies to a power source. This way, if one power supply fails, the other power supply can continue powering the server's uninterrupted operation. For added redundancy, data centers with two separate sources of power can connect each power supply to a different power source.

Data centers also use *uninterruptible power supplies (UPS)*, such as the one shown in Figure 8.6, to provide battery power to systems in the event of a brief disruption. These power sources may also be served by a generator that provides long-term backup power.

Managed *power distribution units (PDUs)* work to manage the power within a rack, ensuring that the power delivered to devices is clean and managed. Additionally, PDUs may support remote management.

Storage

The second priority of many fault tolerance efforts is to protect against the failure of a single storage device. This is achieved through the use of a technology known as *redundant arrays of inexpensive disks (RAID)*. RAID comes in several different forms, but each of them is designed to provide redundancy by having more disks than needed to meet business needs. Let's look at two RAID technologies: disk mirroring and disk striping with parity.

Disk Mirroring

The most basic form of RAID, known as RAID Level 1, is *disk mirroring*. In this approach, the server contains two disks. Each disk has identical contents, and when the system writes any data to one disk, it automatically makes the same changes to the other disk, keeping it as a synchronized copy, or mirror, of the primary disk. If the primary disk fails, the system can automatically switch to the backup disk and continue operating.

F I G U R E   8 . 6   Uninterruptible power supply (UPS)
Source: Sergey Ryzhov/Adobe Stock Photos

You can see this in Figure 8.7. Each of the data blocks A1 through A4 is stored on both disk 0 and disk 1, so that disk 0 and disk 1 are identical.

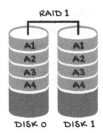

FIGURE 8.7 **RAID 1 disk mirroring**

Disk Striping with Parity

The second major RAID technology is *disk striping with parity*, known as RAID Level 5. In this approach, the system contains three or more disks and writes data across all of those disks but includes additional elements known as parity blocks spread across the disks, as shown in Figure 8.8. If one of the disks fails, the system can regenerate its contents by using that parity information.

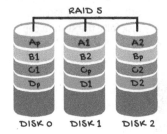

FIGURE 8.8 **RAID 5 disk striping with parity**

Examining Figure 8.8, you can see that sections of each block are stored on two of the three disks, and the third disk contains the parity information for that block. For example, pieces of block A (A2 and A3) are stored on disks 1 and 2, while disk 0 contains the parity information for that block (Ap). Similarly, pieces of block B (B1 and B2) are stored on disks 0 and 1, with the parity information (Bp) stored on disk 2.

> **EXAM TIP**
>
> One important thing to remember: RAID is a fault tolerance strategy designed to protect against a single or double disk failure, depending on the RAID level. It is *not* a backup strategy. You should still perform regular data backups to protect your organization's information in the event of a more catastrophic failure, such as the physical destruction of the entire server.

Networking Components

Networking components also can be single points of failure. Therefore, organizations should consider implementing redundancy at different points in the network. This ranges from having multiple Internet service providers entering a facility to using dual network interface cards in critical servers, similar to the way that we use multiple power supplies. Using two network interface cards is known as *NIC teaming*.

Within a network, add redundancy to critical network paths as well. For example, the connection between servers and their storage is crucial to the operation of the data center. *Multipath* approaches create redundancy in these paths and ensure continuous access to storage.

Redundancy Through Diversity

Finally, at a higher level, think about adding diversity to your environment wherever possible to avoid redundant elements all falling victim to the same flaw at the same time.

Use diverse technologies from a diverse set of vendors to avoid the failure of one technology or vendor from critically impacting your environment. You should also consider diversifying your cryptography and other security controls.

EXAM ESSENTIALS

▶ Business continuity efforts are activities designed to keep a business running in the face of adversity. The business impact analysis (BIA) is an impact assessment that begins by identifying the organization's mission-essential functions and then tracing those backward to identify the critical IT systems that support those processes.

▶ Single point of failure analyses identify places where the failure of one component could cause an entire system or service to become unavailable.

▶ High availability (HA) uses multiple systems to protect against failures. Fault tolerance (FT) helps to protect a single system from failing in the first place by making it resilient in the face of technical failures.

▶ Three of the components most likely to fail in a computer system are the power supply, storage, and network connection.

Practice Question 1

Renee would like to add fault tolerance to the storage capacity of a new server that she is building. She would like to use RAID 5 to protect this server. What is the smallest number of physical disks that she can use?

A. 1
B. 2
C. 3
D. 5

Practice Question 2

Kevin is designing a new web server environment for his organization. He believes that the service will need three servers to support normal traffic levels and decides to use three servers to meet that need. As requests come in, they will be sent to the server that has the most available capacity. Which term best describes what Kevin is doing?

A. Fault tolerance
B. High availability
C. Dual power supplies
D. Load balancing

Practice Question 1 Explanation

RAID 5, also known as disk striping with parity, uses three or more disks and writes data across all of those disks but includes additional elements known as parity blocks spread across the disks. If one of the disks fails, the system can regenerate its contents by using that parity information. Therefore, the minimum number of disks required is three.

It is not possible to use one or two disks with RAID 5 because the data must be spread across two disks and then an additional disk is needed for the parity information.

It is possible to use RAID 5 with five disks, but that is more than the minimum necessary to support the technology.

Correct Answer: C. 3

Practice Question 2 Explanation

Load balancing uses multiple systems to spread the burden of providing service across those systems, providing a scalable computing environment. Kevin is adding multiple servers that will share the load, so he is achieving load balancing.

If Kevin were to add more servers than necessary, that would be high availability. For example, if there were four servers, the environment would still be able to meet the full demand even if one of those servers failed. Since Kevin is only adding the three servers required to meet the load, this situation does not meet the definition of high availability.

Fault tolerance is when you add redundant components to a single server to reduce the likelihood that it will fail. Dual power supplies are an example of fault tolerance. The question does not mention dual power supplies or any other fault tolerance technology.

Correct Answer: D. Load balancing

CHAPTER 9

Disaster Recovery
Objective 2.2 Understand Disaster Recovery (DR)

Business continuity programs are designed to keep a business up and running in the face of a disaster. Unfortunately, however, they may not be effective in certain circumstances. Sometimes continuity controls fail or the sheer magnitude of a disaster overwhelms the organization's capacity to continue operations. That's where disaster recovery begins.

In this chapter, you'll learn about CC objective 2.2. The following subobjectives are covered in this chapter:

▶ **Purpose**
▶ **Importance**
▶ **Components**

DISASTER RECOVERY PLANNING

Disaster recovery (DR) is a subset of business continuity activities designed to restore a business to normal operations as quickly as possible following a disruption. Disaster recovery plans (DRPs) may include immediate measures that get operations working again temporarily, but the disaster recovery efforts are not finished until the organization is completely back to normal.

Types of Disasters

The disaster recovery plan can be triggered by an environmental natural disaster, such as a hurricane, a technological failure, such as a power outage, a health emergency, such as a pandemic, or a hazard caused by humans, such as a ransomware attack.

The source of a disaster or hazard may be internal to the organization, such as a data center failure, or external, such as a supply chain disruption. In any case, the organization must quickly recognize the circumstances and activate its corresponding disaster recovery plan.

Initial Response

Once a disaster recovery plan is activated, the initial response following an emergency disruption is designed to contain the damage to the organization and recover whatever capacity may be immediately restored.

The activities during this initial response will vary widely depending on the nature of the disaster. They may include activating an alternate processing facility, containing physical damage, and calling in contractors to begin an emergency response.

Staffing

During a disaster recovery effort, the focus of most of the organization shifts from normal business activity to a concentrated effort to restore operations as quickly as possible. From a staffing perspective, this means that many employees will be working in temporary jobs that may be completely different from their normally assigned duties. Flexibility is key during a disaster response. Also, the organization should plan out disaster responsibilities as much as possible in advance and provide employees with training that prepares them to do their part during disaster recovery.

Communication

Communication is crucial to disaster recovery efforts. Responders must have secure, reliable means to communicate with each other and the organization's leadership. This includes the initial communication required to activate the disaster recovery process, even if the disaster occurs after hours, regular status updates for both employees in the field and leadership, and ad hoc communications to meet tactical needs.

Assessment

After the immediate danger to the organization clears, the disaster recovery team shifts from initial response mode into assessment mode. The goal of this phase is simple—to triage the damage to the organization and implement functional recovery plans to recover operations on a continuous basis. In some circumstances, it may also include intermediate steps that restore operations temporarily on the way to sustainable and stable recovery.

Disaster Recovery Metrics

The following three metrics are used to help an organization plan disaster recovery efforts:

▶ The *recovery time objective (RTO)* is the targeted amount of time that it will take to restore a service to operation following a disruption.

▶ The organization must also think about the amount of data that it needs to restore. The *recovery point objective (RPO)* is the maximum time period from which data may be lost as a result of a disaster.

▶ The *recovery service level (RSL)* is the percentage of a service that must be available during a disaster. For example, you might set the RSL for your website at 50 percent, recognizing that diminished capacity is acceptable during a disaster response.

Together, the RTO, RPO, and RSL provide valuable information to disaster recovery planners.

> **EXAM TIP**
>
> Remember, disaster recovery efforts conclude only when the organization is back to normal operations in its primary operating environment.

Training and Awareness

Training and awareness efforts are critical components of a disaster recovery plan. All personnel involved in disaster recovery efforts should receive periodic training about their role in the plan. They should also engage in more frequent awareness programs designed to keep their disaster recovery responsibilities top-of-mind.

BACKUPS

Backups are perhaps the most important component of any disaster recovery plan because most businesses today are built around their data. Whether it's proprietary designs, confidential customer lists, or information databases, data drives businesses. For many organizations, the complete loss of data would be a disaster of tremendous proportions.

Backups provide organizations with a fail-safe way to recover their data in the event of a technology failure, human error, natural disaster, or other circumstances that result in its accidental or intentional deletion or modification. Backups are a crucial safety net for data-driven businesses.

Backup Media

Organizations can back up their data in many ways. The simplest approach is to copy files from one location to another, but it is manual and error-prone. Most organizations use a more sophisticated backup strategy.

Tape Backups

Traditionally, organizations wrote their backups to magnetic tapes, and this is still a very common practice today. Linear Tape-Open (LTO) tapes, such as those shown in Figure 9.1, are commonly used for this purpose. However, tapes are difficult to manage, and modern backup approaches often use alternative storage that has become much less expensive over the past few years.

FIGURE 9.1 **LTO backup tapes**
Source: bigmagic/Adobe Stock Photos

Disk Backups

Some organizations do *disk-to-disk backups*, which write data from the primary disk to special disks set aside for backup purposes. These backup disks may be in a separate facility where it would be unlikely that the same physical disaster would affect both the primary and backup sites. Backups that are sent to a storage area network (SAN) or network attached storage (NAS) also fall within this category.

Cloud Backups

A newer trend in backups is to write backups directly to storage provided by cloud computing vendors, such as Amazon Web Services (AWS), Microsoft Azure, or their competitors. Cloud-based storage provides great geographic diversity, as the backup data is stored in separately managed facilities and cloud providers usually perform their own backups of their systems, providing an added layer of protection for customer data.

Backup Types

There are three primary backup types—full, differential, and incremental. They differ based on the data they include.

Full Backups

Full backups, as the name implies, include everything on the media being backed up. They make a complete copy of the data.

Snapshots are a form of full backup created using specialized functionality of the hardware platform. For example, virtualization systems often provide snapshotting capability that allows administrators to quickly create a backup disk image.

Differential and Incremental Backups

Differential backups supplement full backups and create a copy of only the data that has changed since the last full backup. *Incremental backups* are similar to differential backups, but with a small twist: They include only those files that have changed since the most recent full or incremental backup.

Backup Scenario

Let's take a quick look at an example. Joe, the storage administrator for his company, performs a full backup of his systems every Sunday afternoon. He then performs differential backups every weekday evening. If the system fails on Friday morning, which backups would he need to restore?

First, Joe needs a base, so he would need to restore the most recent full backup, from Sunday evening.

Next, Joe needs to retrieve the data that changed since Sunday. Because Joe is using differential backups, each differential backup contains all of the data changed since the last full backup, so Joe only needs to restore the most recent differential backup—the one from Thursday evening.

What if we changed this question a bit and switched Joe's strategy from daily differential backups to daily incremental backups? Now, Joe has a different situation on his hands. Incremental backups are smaller than differential backups and contain only those files that have changed since the most recent full *or* incremental backup.

So, Joe begins the same way, by restoring Sunday's full backup. But then he must apply each incremental backup, in order, that took place since the full backup. This means that he must apply the incremental backups from Monday, Tuesday, Wednesday, and Thursday. It takes a longer time to restore from incremental backups because of this process, but the trade-off is that incremental backups consume less space than differential backups.

DISASTER RECOVERY SITES

During a disaster, organizations may need to shift their computing functions from their primary data center to an alternate facility designed to carry the load when the primary site is unavailable or nonfunctioning. Disaster recovery sites are alternate processing facilities specifically designed for this purpose.

Most of the time, disaster recovery sites sit idle, waiting to step in when an emergency situation arises. There are three main types of alternate processing facilities:

- ▶ Hot sites
- ▶ Cold sites
- ▶ Warm sites

Hot Sites

Hot sites are the premier form of alternate processing facility. They are fully operational data centers that have all of the equipment and data required to handle operations ready to run.

Technology staff can activate the hot site within a moment's notice, and in many cases, the hot site will activate itself if the primary site fails. This provides an unparalleled level of redundancy, but it also comes at great expense. The costs of building and maintaining a hot site are typically similar to those of running the primary data center. You're doubling your costs to achieve tremendous recovery ability.

Cold Sites

Cold sites are facilities that can be used to restore operations eventually, but with a significant investment of time. They're essentially empty data centers. They have the core racks, cabling, network connections, and environmental controls necessary to support data center operations, but don't have the servers or data required to restore business operations.

Cold sites are far less expensive than hot sites, but activating them can take weeks or even months.

Warm Sites

Warm sites are a compromise. They do have the hardware and software necessary to support the company's operations, but they are not kept running in a parallel fashion. The hardware costs are the same as a hot site, but much less investment of time from IT staff is required.

Activating a warm site can take hours or days, depending on the circumstances.

Offsite Storage

Disaster recovery sites not only provide a facility for technology operations but also serve as an offsite storage location for business data.

Backing up business data is important, and storing those backups in a secure facility that is geographically distant from the primary facility provides added assurance that the same disaster will not damage both the primary facility and the backups. This is all part of performing a site risk assessment as you select locations. This process is known as *site resiliency*.

Backups may be physically transported to the disaster recovery site on a periodic basis, or they may be transferred digitally using a process known as site replication, using features built in to an organization's storage or virtual machine platform.

When planning backup storage at offsite facilities, you'll want to make a strategic choice whether these backups are kept in an online or offline format. Online backups are available for restoration at a moment's notice, but they require a significant financial investment. Offline backups may require manual intervention to restore, but they are much less expensive.

Alternate Business Processes

In addition to alternate processing facilities, organizations can incorporate alternate business processes as a component of their disaster recovery plans. For example, an organization might move to manual processes such as a paper-based ordering process if the electronic order management system will remain down for an extended period. Alternate business processes allow businesses to remain flexible in the event of a disaster.

TESTING DISASTER RECOVERY PLANS

Disaster recovery plans are critical to ensuring the continuity of business operations. Like any security control, they should be tested to ensure that they function effectively and will be ready to restore business operations in the event of a disruption. Each test of a disaster recovery plan has the following two goals:

1. To validate that the plan functions correctly and that the technology will work in the event of a disaster
2. To provide an opportunity to identify necessary updates to the plan due to technology or business process changes

There are five major types of disaster recovery tests: read-throughs, walk-throughs, simulations, parallel tests, and full interruption tests.

Read-Throughs

Read-throughs are the simplest form of disaster recovery testing. They're also known as checklist reviews. In this approach, disaster recovery staff distribute copies of the current plan to all personnel involved in disaster recovery efforts and ask them to review their procedures. Team members then provide feedback about any updates needed to keep the plan current.

Walk-Throughs

Walk-throughs go a step further and involve getting everyone together around the same table to review the plan together. For this reason, the walk-through is also known as a tabletop exercise. Walk-throughs achieve the same result as read-throughs but are generally more effective because they give the team the opportunity to discuss the plan together.

Simulations

The next level of disaster recovery testing is the *simulation test*. As with the structured walk-through, the simulation pulls together the disaster recovery team. The difference is that in the simulation they're not just talking about the plan; they are discussing how they would respond in a specific scenario. The test planners design a simulation of an emergency situation and then the disaster recovery team describes how they would react.

Parallel Tests

The three test types discussed so far—read-throughs, walk-throughs, and simulations—are all theoretical exercises. They talk about disaster recovery but don't actually use any

DR technology. The *parallel test* goes beyond this and actually activates the DR plan, including activating an alternate cloud or physical operating environment in response to a simulated disaster. A company doesn't actually switch operations to the backup environment, but the DR environment runs in parallel with the primary site.

Full Interruption Tests

The final test, the *full interruption test*, is the most effective type of DR test; however, it is also the most disruptive to normal operations. The business simulates a disaster by actually shutting down the primary operating environment and attempting to operate out of the DR environment. This test type will highlight any deficiencies in the plan, but it could also have an adverse effect on the business. For this reason, full interruption tests are rare.

Disaster recovery testing strategies often use a combination of different test types. An organization might conduct regular read-throughs and walk-throughs of the plan and supplement them with periodic simulations and parallel tests. Each test type brings distinct benefits and helps the organization prepare for an actual disaster.

EXAM ESSENTIALS

▶ Disaster recovery (DR) is a subset of business continuity activities designed to restore a business to normal operations as quickly as possible following a disruption.

▶ The recovery time objective (RTO) is the targeted amount of time that it will take to restore a service to operation following a disruption. The recovery point objective (RPO) is the maximum time period from which data may be lost as a result of a disaster. The recovery service level (RSL) is the percentage of a service that must be available during a disaster.

▶ Full backups include everything on the media being backed up. They make a complete copy of the data. Snapshots are a form of full backup created using specialized functionality of the hardware platform. Differential backups supplement full backups and create a copy of only the data that has changed since the last full backup. Incremental backups include only those files that have changed since the most recent full or incremental backup.

▶ Hot sites are fully operational data centers that have all the equipment and data required to handle operations ready to run. Cold sites are facilities that can be used to restore operations eventually, but they are essentially empty office spaces. Warm sites have the hardware and software necessary to support the company's operations, but they are not kept running in a parallel fashion.

Practice Question 1

Gene recently conducted an assessment and determined that his organization can be without its main transaction database for a maximum of 2 hours before unacceptable damage occurs to the business. Therefore, the goal of his organization is to restore service within 2 hours. Which metric has Gene identified?

A. RSL
B. RTO
C. RPO
D. MTTR

Practice Question 2

Which type of recovery site has some or most systems in place but does not have the data needed to take over operations?

A. Hot site
B. Warm site
C. Cloud site
D. Cold site

Practice Question 1 Explanation

The recovery time objective (RTO) is the time-based goal for restoring service after a disruption. Gene is setting the RTO at 2 hours to meet his organization's business needs.

The recovery point objective (RPO) is the maximum time period from which data may be lost as a result of a disaster, not the goal for restoring service.

The recovery service level (RSL) is the percentage of a service that must be available during a disaster, not the amount of time that may be taken to restore service.

The mean time to repair (MTTR) is the average amount of time required to repair a device and is not a goal for future recovery efforts.

Correct Answer: B. RTO

Practice Question 2 Explanation

Warm sites have systems, connectivity, and power, but they do not have the up-to-the-minute data to immediately take over operations.

A hot site can immediately take over operations, whereas a cold site has the space, power, and likely connectivity but requires systems and data to be put in place before use.

Cloud sites are not one of the three common types of recovery sites.

Correct Answer: B. Warm site

CHAPTER 10

Incident Response

Objective 2.3 Understand Incident Response

While we strive to protect our systems and information against a wide variety of threats, the grim reality is that no matter how many controls we put in place, there's still a possibility that we'll fall victim to a security incident. Cybersecurity professionals must have plans and procedures to handle these incidents when they arise.

In this chapter, you'll learn about CC objective 2.3. The following subobjectives are covered in this chapter:

▶ **Purpose**
▶ **Importance**
▶ **Components**

CREATING AN INCIDENT RESPONSE PROGRAM

This section explores the *incident response* process, focusing on a standard incident response process endorsed by the National Institute of Standards and Technology (NIST), as shown in Figure 10.1. It uses the following phases:

> ▶ *Preparation*, which includes the activities used to put together an incident response plan and team
> ▶ *Detection & Analysis*, which identifies that an incident is taking place and determines the extent of the incident's impact

► *Containment, Eradication & Recovery*, which limits the damage caused by an incident, removes the effects of the incident, and restores normal operations

► *Post-incident Activity*, which analyzes the response process and identifies lessons learned to improve future response efforts

This process is fully described in the *NIST Computer Security Incident Handling Guide* (NIST SP 800-61). This document is widely used as a standard reference throughout the cybersecurity field.

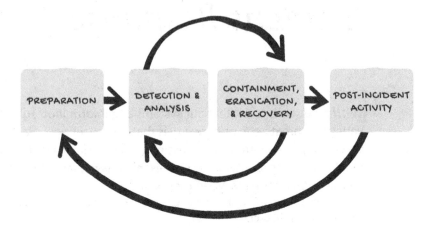

FIGURE 10.1 **NIST incident response life cycle**

Every organization should develop a cybersecurity incident response plan that outlines the policies, procedures, and guidelines the organization will follow when an incident takes place. This preparation process is extremely important because it provides structure and organization during a crisis.

THE IMPORTANCE OF PLANNING

I've been involved in many security incidents throughout my career. In hindsight, it's clear that all the organizations that handled incidents well had one thing in common: They had thought through their incident response process and documented it in advance. On the other hand, when I think about the incidents that didn't go very well, they typically occurred in organizations that didn't conduct prior planning. In those organizations, I commonly heard the sentiment, "Well, we're good at crisis management, and a security incident isn't that likely. We'll figure out the details when it happens."

That seat-of-the-pants approach to cybersecurity incident handling is a recipe for failure. The reality is that people make bad decisions in the heat of a crisis. Developing an incident response plan in advance of an incident taking place allows you to make decisions in the calm environment of a planning phase, which then helps you exercise good judgment in the heat of an incident.

A formalized incident response plan should include several common elements:

▶ It should begin with a *statement of purpose*. Why is the organization creating an incident response plan, and what is its scope? Which types of incidents does the plan cover? For example, is it restricted to only cybersecurity incidents, or does it cover any loss of sensitive information?

▶ It should describe *clear strategies and goals* for the incident response effort. What are the highest priorities for first responders and those handling an incident at a more strategic level? If responders should prioritize containment over evidence preservation, make sure that's clear in the plan.

▶ It should describe the nature of the *organization's approach to incident response*. Who is responsible for incident handling? What authority do they have?

▶ It should also cover *communication* within the team, with other groups within the organization, and with third parties.

▶ It should include the *approval of senior management*. You might need that authority when taking unpopular actions during incident response. If you can point to the plan and show an irate administrator that the policy requiring disconnection of a system was signed by the CEO, that goes a long way.

As you develop your plan, you should consult NIST SP 800-61 to help guide your decisions. You also might find it helpful to look at some plans developed by other organizations. Of course, you won't be able to simply take someone else's plan and apply it to your organization, but it's always helpful to have a starting point. Many cybersecurity professionals have put countless hours into developing strong incident response plans, and there's no need to reinvent the wheel.

BUILDING AN INCIDENT RESPONSE TEAM

One of the most important tasks that you'll undertake in your incident response program is to build and staff your incident response team.

This team will likely need to be available on a 24/7 basis, and you should have primary and backup personnel assigned to cover vacations as well as extended periods of operation. Incident handling is a wonderful professional development opportunity and helps team members keep their technical skills sharp.

Team Composition

Some of the groups that should be represented in your incident response team include the following:

- ▶ Management
- ▶ Information security personnel
- ▶ Physical security team members
- ▶ Technical subject matter experts, such as database administrators, developers, systems engineers, and virtualization experts
- ▶ Legal counsel
- ▶ Public relations and marketing staff
- ▶ Human resources team members

Including the right team members is critical to building the relationships that you'll need during an incident. You won't necessarily need to activate all team members for any given incident, but each of these groups should have representatives trained and ready to participate before an incident strikes.

As you build out your incident response team, you may find that your organization lacks some of the capacity to handle security incidents. For example, you might discover that you don't have the forensic capabilities within your team to conduct investigations in support of incident response efforts. In those cases, you may want to consider retaining an external incident response provider to assist.

> **EXAM TIP**
>
> You don't want to try to locate and negotiate a contract with a provider in the middle of an incident. Plan in advance, and get the paperwork in place to use a provider immediately when you discover a problem. Your incident response team will be a crucial asset as you work to address the impact of a security incident. Be sure that you take the time now to design and train your team, so that they're ready to respond in the event of an actual cybersecurity incident.

Training and Testing

Once your team is in place, you should work with them regularly. Don't wait until incidents occur to pull everyone together. Provide them with your incident response plan documentation and conduct regular training and testing to ensure that they work well together and are ready to react quickly in the event of an incident.

INCIDENT COMMUNICATIONS PLAN

One of the critical components of your incident response program is an *incident communications plan* that covers both internal and external communications. A good incident communications plan is a crucial element of stakeholder management.

Internal Communications

Incident notification and escalation procedures help ensure that the appropriate people within your organization know about an incident at the right time and are provided with the right information.

External Communications

Communicating with individuals and groups outside of your organization can be a much trickier task. Clearly, you want to make sure that you're limiting the communication of sensitive information to trusted parties. This is particularly important when there might be public or media interest in an incident. If word leaks out without approval, the incident might wind up in the news before your public relations team is ready to handle it. This might also jeopardize the integrity of your investigation by alerting attackers to the fact that you've discovered the incident and an incident response effort is underway.

In most cases, you aren't under a legal obligation to report security incidents to law enforcement, and the decision to do so is complex. Once you file a report with law enforcement, it's likely that details of the incident will become public, which may be undesirable. Also, law enforcement officials are held to much higher standards in gathering and processing evidence. Of course, you should always contact law enforcement if you think there is a threat to safety or you have a legal obligation to report a specific kind of incident.

Your legal team should be included in your incident response planning efforts. They should provide you with specific guidance about any laws or regulations that apply to your organization and may require notification in the event of a security incident. For example, most states have privacy laws that require the timely notification of individuals when there is a compromise of personal information. You may also have obligations under other laws and regulations to notify government agencies, private regulatory bodies, customers, or the public about specific types of incidents, depending on their impact and the types of information involved.

Secure Communications

Your communications plan should not only describe *who* you will communicate with during an incident but should also describe *how* you will communicate. Make sure that you have secure communications paths in place, before an incident occurs, that provide you with confidential mechanisms to share information with trusted employees and third parties. Using secure channels prevents the inadvertent release of information to the public or adversaries.

INCIDENT IDENTIFICATION AND RESPONSE

Once you have an incident response plan in place and a team prepared, the incident response process enters a state of perpetual monitoring: watching for signs that an incident is taking place or has already occurred. There are many different ways that an organization might identify a security incident.

Security Data Sources

The key to successful incident identification is to have a robust security monitoring infrastructure. Data is crucial to incident detection and organizations have a responsibility to collect, analyze, and retain security information.

Many information sources can contribute data crucial to identifying and analyzing a possible security incident, including:

- ▶ Intrusion detection and prevention systems
- ▶ Firewalls
- ▶ Authentication systems
- ▶ System integrity monitors
- ▶ Vulnerability scanners
- ▶ System event logs
- ▶ NetFlow connection records
- ▶ Antimalware packages

If IT systems do one thing well, it's generating massive amounts of log information!

Correlating Security Information

Security professionals are responsible for collecting and correlating log information. Unassisted, that's almost an impossible undertaking. Fortunately, *security information and event management (SIEM)* technology can assist with this task. SIEM systems act as centralized log repository and analysis solutions. Security professionals can take the firehose of data they receive from security-related logs and point it at the SIEM, which can then do the heavy lifting of analysis. SIEM systems can detect possible incidents based on rules and algorithms, bringing them to the attention of security administrators for further review. They also provide a critical centralized information source to investigators pursuing a security incident.

Receiving Incident Reports

I've just discussed many of the ways that a security team might identify incidents based on internally generated data, and, in the best case, that's the way security professionals detect incidents—by noticing the signs of an incident as it occurs or shortly thereafter. Unfortunately, sometimes those monitoring systems fail to detect an incident and we first learn of a security compromise by hearing from employees, customers, or external organizations who see the signs of a breach. This might occur because a customer sees their personal information posted on the web, because a system on the corporate network begins attacking an external site due to commands received from a botnet, or because an employee notices being unable to log in to an email account. The incident response team should have a consistent method for receiving, recording, and evaluating these reports.

Responding to Incidents

When a security professional identifies a potential incident, it's time to swing into incident response mode. The team member who first notices an incident and others who may be on duty have special first responder responsibilities. Just as in a medical emergency, the first person on the scene can have a tremendous impact on the successful response to an incident by acting quickly and decisively to protect the organization.

First responders should act quickly to contain the damage from a security incident. If they suspect that a system or group of systems may be compromised, they should isolate that system from the remainder of the network to contain the damage. Depending on the technical circumstances, they may quarantine the system by removing it from the network, keeping it running to preserve evidence but cutting off the potentially compromised system's ability to communicate with attackers or infect other systems on the corporate network.

> **EXAM TIP**
>
> This is a favorite topic for exam questions. Remember that a first responder's highest priority should be containing the damage by isolating affected systems.

As you are building out your incident response capabilities, be sure to integrate them with your threat intelligence program as well. Organizations with strong strategic intelligence programs will be able to more rapidly and effectively identify potential incidents.

At the same time, remember that your adversaries are gathering intelligence on your organization and its operations as well. Counterintelligence programs are designed to thwart these efforts by denying adversaries access to intelligence or deliberately feeding them misinformation.

EXAM ESSENTIALS

▶ The four stages of the NIST incident response process are preparation, detection & analysis, containment, eradication & recovery, and post-incident activity.

▶ Incident response teams commonly include members from management, information security, physical security, legal counsel, public relations, human resources, along with technical subject matter experts.

▶ The highest priority of a first responder during incident response is to quickly contain the damage caused by the security incident.

▶ Security information and event management (SIEM) systems act as centralized log repository and analysis solutions.

Practice Question 1

Jason is monitoring his organization's SIEM system watching for signs of unusual activity. Which phase of the NIST incident response process best describes his work?

A. Preparation
B. Detection & analysis
C. Post-incident activity
D. Containment, eradication & recovery

Practice Question 2

During his monitoring work, Jason identifies a high-priority security incident in progress. What should be his first priority?

A. Identifying lessons learned
B. Notifying senior management
C. Recovering normal operations
D. Containing the damage

Practice Question 1 Explanation

Jason is monitoring his environment for signs of unusual activity. This is an activity designed to identify security incidents and, therefore, belongs to the detection & analysis phase of the incident response process.

The preparation phase includes the activities used to put together an incident response program and team.

The containment, eradication, and recovery phase limits the damage caused by an incident, removes the effects of the incident, and restores normal operations.

The post-incident activity phase analyzes the response process and identifies lessons learned to improve future response efforts.

Correct Answer: B. Detection & analysis

Practice Question 2 Explanation

This is a tricky question because Jason and the incident response team will likely take all of these actions during the incident response effort. The key to answering this question correctly is to notice that it is asking for the first priority.

The first priority of any incident response effort should always be to contain the damage. Jason should immediately take steps to isolate any affected systems to stop the spread of the incident.

Notifying senior management and activating the incident response process is also a high priority, but Jason should first take immediate action to contain the damage. If other team members are available, he can ask them to perform notification and escalation while he is containing the damage.

Recovering normal operations and identifying lessons learned come much later in the process, after the initial emergency has been resolved.

Correct Answer: D. Containing the damage

PART III

Domain 3: Access Controls Concepts

Chapter 11 Physical Access Controls
Chapter 12 Logical Access Controls

Access Controls Concepts is the third domain of ISC2's Certified in Cybersecurity exam. It provides the knowledge that entry-level cybersecurity professionals need to know about restricting access to systems and data. This domain includes the following two objectives:

3.1 Understand physical access controls
3.2 Understand logical access controls

Questions from this domain make up 22 percent of the questions on the CC exam, so you should expect to see 22 questions on your test covering the material in this part.

CHAPTER 11

Physical Access Controls
Objective 3.1 Understand Physical Access Controls

Cybersecurity professionals must ensure the physical security of the facilities under their control. This includes limiting access to those facilities, authenticating employees seeking to gain access, and tracking contractors and other visitors who access the site.

In this chapter, you'll learn about CC objective 3.1. The following subobjectives are covered in this chapter:

▶ **Physical security controls (e.g., badge systems, gate entry, environmental design)**
▶ **Monitoring (e.g., security guards, closed-circuit television (CCTV), alarm systems, logs)**
▶ **Authorized versus unauthorized personnel**

PHYSICAL FACILITIES

Let's begin the discussion of physical security by discussing some of the different types of facilities that must be protected.

Data Centers

Data centers are the most obvious locations of concern to cybersecurity professionals. These secure facilities, such as the one shown in Figure 11.1, contain all of the servers, storage, and other computing resources needed to run our business. Data center access must be strictly limited to prevent the potential theft of resources and information.

Anyone gaining physical access to a data center would have the ability to cause significant damage and disruption to the business.

FIGURE 11.1 **A typical data center facility**
Source: .shock/Adobe Stock Photos

Server Rooms

Not all servers are kept within the relatively safe confines of a managed data center. Some businesses only have simple *server rooms*, which often lack strong security controls. These server rooms may also proliferate within business units of organizations that have central data centers because they tend to pop up organically, beginning with just a few servers in a room and growing until they may have the capacity of small data centers.

Media Storage Facilities

Media storage facilities also require security attention. Good disaster recovery and business continuity plans place copies of critical business information, including system backups, at remote locations. These locations contain sensitive data and must have security standards equal to or even greater than the main data center, due to their remote locations.

Evidence Storage Rooms

Cybersecurity professionals often engage in digital forensic investigations. If evidence handled during these investigations may be used in court, investigators must document and preserve the chain of custody, ensuring that evidence is not tampered with while under their care. This requires secure *evidence storage rooms* that are safe from intrusion.

Wiring Closets

Wiring closets, such as the one shown in Figure 11.2, are often overlooked as a physical security concern. They exist throughout an organization's buildings, and if they're not properly secured, they can offer an intruder physical access to eavesdrop on network communications or gain access to sensitive networks.

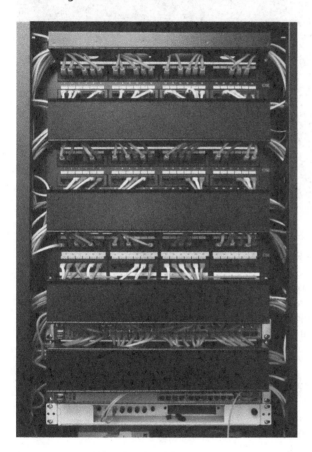

FIGURE 11.2 A wiring closet

Source: Ken MacDougall/Adobe Stock Photos

The need for protection extends to *cable distribution runs* that leave wiring closets and then travel around an organization's facility to deliver network connectivity, such as the one shown in Figure 11.3.

FIGURE 11.3 **Cable distribution runs**
Source: JIRMoronta/Adobe Stock Photos

There may be other secure areas of a business that require similar protections. These include security and network operation centers (SOCs and NOCs) and other restricted work areas. Security professionals should perform an inventory of all sensitive locations under their control and conduct physical security assessments of those facilities.

DESIGNING FOR SECURITY

Developing a strong physical security program is not just an IT problem. Physical security affects the physical world, and the way that your facilities are designed and placed can affect how well they can be secured.

Placing facilities in areas where there is plenty of pedestrian and vehicle traffic makes it much less likely that an intruder is going to try to break in because it increases the chance that they will be caught. Even using signs warning people that they are being monitored and are nearing a secured area can help deter attacks.

Facility designers can use pedestrian and vehicle gates to limit the number of places where a person can enter a facility. This allows you to focus your security attention on those access points with security guards, alarm systems, closed-circuit television cameras, and similar controls.

If you're trying to prevent vehicles from entering an area, physical barriers known as *bollards* can be used to block sidewalks and access roads. Some bollards, such as the ones shown in Figure 11.4, are retractable so that authorized vehicles can enter an area.

FIGURE 11.4 **Bollards used to block vehicle access**

Source: Kirill Gorlov/Adobe Stock Photos

Physical security experts often adopt a strategy called *crime prevention through environmental design (CPTED)* to help focus their work. This approach promotes designing facilities to achieve the following three main goals:

1. *Natural surveillance*: This means that facilities are designed in such a way that allows employees and passersby to observe what is happening around the facility and notice a potential intruder. You can achieve natural surveillance by placing windows appropriately, creating open areas around fences, and using adequate lighting.
2. *Natural access control*: This uses gates and other structures to funnel people into a single point of entry and limits the ability of an intruder to get to areas where they might not be under surveillance.
3. *Natural territorial reinforcement*: This strategy makes it obvious that an area is closed to the public through signage, landscaping, lighting, and similar techniques.

CPTED strategies increase the physical security of a facility by reducing the risk of a successful intrusion.

VISITOR MANAGEMENT

Occasionally you will need to allow visitors to access your secured facilities. It is important to have visitor control procedures in place that describe who can authorize visitor access and how visitors can behave in your facilities.

Your visitor access procedures should clearly identify the allowable reasons that a visitor might access your facilities and the appropriate levels of approval required for different types of visitors in different circumstances. They should also explain what types of visitors, if any, may be granted unescorted access to the facility and who may escort other visitors.

Each time a visitor enters a secure facility, you should maintain a log of that access. This may be as simple as having visitors sign a paper visitor register, or it may use a more complex electronic process.

All individuals inside a secure facility should wear identification badges that are clearly displayed on their person. Badges for visitors should be distinctive enough that employees can quickly recognize whether someone they encounter is a fellow employee or a visitor. If a visitor is not allowed unescorted access to the facility, the badge should clearly indicate that an escort is required.

Cameras may be used to provide an added level of monitoring to areas where visitors are present. The use of *closed-circuit television (CCTV) cameras* should always be disclosed to visitors. Camera footage can be consulted later if any suspicious activity occurred during a visit.

PHYSICAL SECURITY PERSONNEL

While technology certainly plays an important role in physical security, physical security programs also often rely on human and automated guards to play a role in securing facilities.

Security Personnel

People often play a role in allowing access to a facility, using human judgment to evaluate visitor requests and grant access to authorized visitors. While many of these procedures can be assisted with technology, there's really no solid substitute for human judgment.

Having human security guards also helps organizations present a welcoming face to the public while protecting their security. To outside visitors, security personnel might seem like mere receptionists, but in reality they are playing a crucial security function.

In environments where an organization wants to make a bold statement about physical security, they may use overt uniformed guards to project an air of security and authority. Depending on local regulations, these guards may be armed.

Security Protocols

The *two-person rule* helps ensure that personnel involved in very sensitive operations act appropriately. This principle comes in the following two forms:

> ▶ *Two-person integrity* requires that two people be present for any access to a sensitive area, such as where valuable items are stored. The presence of two

people deters theft or other unauthorized activity by a single person, requiring that they collude with a second individual to carry out illicit activity.

▶ *Two-person control* is slightly different. It is used to control access to very sensitive functions, requiring the concurrence of two individuals to carry out an action.

The most common example of two-person control is the use of two keys to launch nuclear missiles. The key mechanisms are located far enough apart from each other that a single person can't reach them both, requiring that two people turn their keys at the same time to trigger a launch.

> **EXAM TIP**
>
> It's very easy to confuse two-person integrity and two-person control. Remember that two-person integrity is about access to sensitive physical facilities, whereas two-person control is about performing sensitive actions.

EXAM ESSENTIALS

▶ Cybersecurity professionals should put controls in place that limit access to sensitive facilities, including data centers, server rooms, media storage facilities, evidence storage rooms, wiring closets, and cable distribution runs.

▶ The three goals of crime prevention through environmental design (CPTED) are natural surveillance, natural access control, and natural territorial reinforcement.

▶ Visitor access to sensitive facilities should be carefully controlled with procedures that describe who can authorize visitor access and how visitors can behave in your facilities. Visitor access should be recorded in a log, and visitors should wear badges that clearly identify their status.

▶ Two-person integrity requires that two people be present for any access to a sensitive area, such as where valuable items are stored. Two-person control is used to control access to very sensitive functions, requiring the concurrence of two individuals to carry out an action.

Practice Question 1

Brynn is responsible for the physical security of a facility that stores backup tapes containing sensitive information. She is implementing a new policy that requires that no employee access the facility alone and that any access requires the presence of at least two authorized employees. Which term best describes this policy?

A. Two-person rule
B. Two-person control
C. Two-person restriction
D. Two-person integrity

Practice Question 2

Which of the following is *not* a goal of the crime prevention through environmental design (CPTED) philosophy?

A. Natural surveillance
B. Natural detection
C. Natural access control
D. Natural territorial reinforcement

Practice Question 1 Explanation

The scenario described here, where two people are required to gain physical access to a sensitive location, is best referred to as two-person integrity.

Two-person integrity is an example of the two-person rule, but two-person integrity is a more specific term and therefore is the better answer.

Two-person control is a different example of the two-person rule that is used to require two people to perform a sensitive process, rather than gaining access to a physical facility.

Two-person restriction is not a commonly used security term.

Correct Answer: D. Two-person integrity

Practice Question 2 Explanation

The three goals of the crime prevention through environmental design (CPTED) philosophy are natural surveillance, natural access control, and natural territorial reinforcement.

Natural detection is not one of the CPTED goals.

Correct Answer: B. Natural detection

CHAPTER 12

Logical Access Controls

Objective 3.2 Understand Logical Access Controls

Chapter 2, "Authentication and Authorization," introduced the access control process and discussed authentication in detail. This chapter explores the authorization and account management process further by examining several common access control models.

In this chapter, you'll learn about CC objective 3.2. The following subobjectives are covered:

- ▶ **Principle of least privilege**
- ▶ **Segregation of duties**
- ▶ **Discretionary access control (DAC)**
- ▶ **Mandatory access control (MAC)**
- ▶ **Role-based access control (RBAC)**

AUTHORIZATION

Authorization is the final step in the access control process. Once someone successfully authenticates to a system, authorization determines the privileges they have to access resources and information.

Least Privilege

Before discussing the different ways to implement authorization, it's important to discuss an underlying principle: the principle of *least privilege*. This principle states that an individual should only have the minimum set of permissions necessary to accomplish their job duties.

Least privilege is important for the following two reasons:

▶ Least privilege minimizes the potential damage from an insider attack. If an employee turns malicious, the damage they can cause will be limited by the privileges assigned to them by job role. It's unlikely, for example, that an accountant would be able to deface the company website, because an accountant's job responsibilities have nothing to do with updating web content.

▶ Least privilege limits the ability of an external attacker to quickly gain privileged access when compromising an employee's account. Unless they happen to compromise a system administrator's account, they will find themselves limited by the privileges of the account that they steal.

Segregation of Duties

The *segregation of duties* principle says that no single person should possess two permissions that, in combination, allow them to perform a sensitive operation. Instead, those permissions should be segregated and held by two different people. Account reviews and audits should inspect permissions to ensure that segregation of duties is properly enforced.

> **EXAM TIP**
>
> Most people in the cybersecurity community refer to this principle as "separation of duties." However, the CC exam objectives specifically use the word "segregation," so be sure to know that terminology as you prepare for the test!

One of the most common requirements for segregation of duties comes in the world of accounting. Organizations normally separate the duties of creating new vendors in their accounting systems and authorizing payments to vendors. This separation prevents a single employee in the accounting department from creating a fake vendor and then issuing payments to that vendor in an attempt to embezzle funds. When segregation of responsibilities is properly implemented, no single employee would be able to create a fake vendor and issue payments to it. Instead, carrying out this theft would require the collusion of two employees with the required privileges. In this case, information security professionals would be responsible for configuring the access control system to prevent violations of segregation of duties.

IT staff can also be the target of segregation of duties controls. In the world of software development, this commonly surfaces as a requirement that developers cannot put their own code into production. Instead, they must submit their code to a testing and evaluation process, and only after it passes rigorous security and functionality checks does a separate person move the code into production.

Authorization Models

The principle of least privilege is used when access control systems are designed that enforce authorization requirements. Several different authorization models are available in these systems.

Mandatory Access Control

Mandatory access control (MAC) systems are the most stringent type of access control. In MAC systems, the operating system itself restricts the permissions that can be granted to users and processes on system resources. Instead, permissions are granted by the systems based on a series of labels placed on users and the objects they want to access. Users and system administrators themselves cannot modify permissions; therefore, MAC is rarely fully implemented on production systems outside of highly secure environments. MAC is normally implemented as a rule-based access control system where users and resources have labels and the operating system makes access control decisions by comparing those labels.

Discretionary Access Control

Discretionary access control (DAC) systems offer a flexible approach to authorization, allowing users to assign access permissions to other users; the owners of files, computers, and other resources have the *discretion* to configure permissions as they see fit for objects that they own. DAC systems are the most common form of access control because they provide organizations with needed flexibility. Imagine if users in your organization didn't have the ability to assign file rights to other users as needed and IT had to be involved in every request. That would certainly make life difficult, wouldn't it?

Most organizations use DAC systems to restrict access to their data. Users who own files, printers, and other resources can grant permission to access those resources to other users. They do this by changing the permissions on an access control list (ACL) for that file, such as the one shown in Figure 12.1.

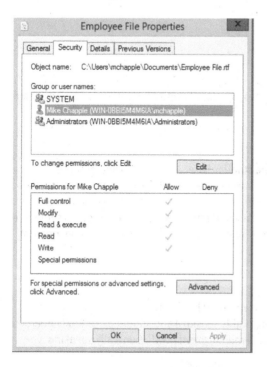

FIGURE 12.1 A Microsoft Windows access control list

Role-Based Access Control

Role-based access control (RBAC) systems simplify some of the work of managing authorizations. Instead of trying to manage all the permissions for an individual user, administrators create job-based roles and then assign permissions to those roles. They can then assign users to roles. This is a little more work up front, but it makes life much easier down the road.

When a new user arrives, the administrator doesn't need to figure out all the explicit permissions that user requires—the user just needs to be assigned to the appropriate roles, and all the appropriate permissions will follow. Similarly, when a group of users needs a new permission, the administrator doesn't have to apply it to each user individually. The new permission can be assigned to the role, and all users with that role will receive the permission automatically.

> **NOTE**
>
> When designing an access control system, you need to select the approaches that best balance security requirements and business needs in your organization. On the one hand, if you choose a system that is not strict enough, you might unintentionally jeopardize your security. On the other hand, however, if you choose a system that is too strict, you might make it too difficult for people to get their work done.

ACCOUNT TYPES

Access control systems contain several types of accounts, and each category requires different types of controls.

User Accounts

Most of the accounts that you manage are standard user accounts. Each account is assigned to an individual user and grants routine access to resources. Everyone from the receptionist to the CEO in an organization typically has a standard user account, even though those accounts may have dramatically different privileges. User accounts should be subject to routine monitoring for compromise and should follow a life cycle management process for creation and removal.

Administrator Accounts

Some accounts belong to system administrators and have extensive privileges to modify system configurations. These accounts are highly sensitive and should be carefully guarded using a process known as *privileged account management (PAM)*. Generally speaking, you should log every action performed by a privileged account and treat any suspicious activity as a high priority for investigation.

It's easy for users with privileged access to make mistakes and cause unintended but drastic consequences. Also, the more that you use an account, the higher the likelihood of compromise. Therefore, administrative users who require privileged access typically have standard user accounts that they use for most of their routine activity and then manually elevate their account to privileged status when they need to issue an administrative command. The exact mechanism for this elevation will vary depending on the access control system, but it may consist of logging in with a different account or assuming an administrative role.

Guest Accounts

Guest accounts provide users with temporary access to resources. For example, you might use guest accounts to grant a visitor access to your wireless network. Guest accounts should be tied to unique individuals and should expire after a reasonable period of time.

Shared/Generic Accounts

Shared or generic accounts are accounts where more than one individual has access to use the account. Generally speaking, these accounts are a bad idea. It is difficult to trace who performed an action with a shared account, and every user has plausible deniability when several people have access to an account.

Service Accounts

Service accounts are a special type of account used internally by a system to run a process or perform other actions. These accounts typically have privileged access and should be carefully controlled. You should configure service accounts so that they cannot be used to log in to the system interactively, and their passwords should not be known by anyone.

NON-REPUDIATION

Another important focus of some security controls is to provide *non-repudiation*. Repudiation is a term that means denying that something is true. Non-repudiation is a security goal that prevents someone from falsely denying that something is true.

For example, you might agree to pay someone $10,000 in exchange for a car. If you just had a handshake agreement, it might be possible for you to later repudiate your actions. You might claim that you never agreed to purchase the car or that you agreed to pay a lower price.

You can solve this issue by using signed contracts when you sell a car. Your signature on the document is the proof that you agreed to the terms. If you later go to court, the person selling you the car can prove that you agreed by showing the judge the signed document. Physical signatures provide non-repudiation on contracts, receipts, and other paper documents.

There's also an electronic form of the physical signature. *Digital signatures* use encryption technology to provide non-repudiation for electronic documents.

There are other ways that you can provide non-repudiation as well. You might use biometric security controls, such as a fingerprint or facial recognition, to prove that someone was in a facility or performed an action. You might also use video surveillance for that same purpose. All of these controls enable you to prove that someone was in a particular location or performed an action, offering some degree of non-repudiation.

EXAM ESSENTIALS

▶ Non-repudiation uses technical measures to ensure that a user is not able to later deny that they took some action.

▶ The principle of least privilege says that users should have only the minimum set of privileges necessary to carry out their job responsibilities.

▶ The segregation of duties principle says that no single person should possess two permissions that, in combination, allow them to perform a sensitive operation.

▶ Mandatory access control (MAC) systems are the most stringent type of access control. In MAC systems, the operating system itself restricts the permissions that may be granted to users and processes on system resources.

▶ Discretionary access control (DAC) systems allow users to assign access permissions to other users—the owners of files, computers, and other resources have the discretion to configure permissions as they see fit.

▶ In role-based access control (RBAC) systems, administrators assign users to roles based upon their job responsibilities and assign the permissions necessary to carry out different jobs to those roles.

Practice Question 1

You are designing an access control system where each file is owned by an individual user and that user decides who can access the file. Which term best describes this access control system?

A. MAC
B. RBAC
C. DAC
D. ABAC

Practice Question 2

You are working with a home loan provider who needs a system that will ensure that they can prove in court that a user signed a contract. What type of requirement are they most directly trying to achieve?

A. Authentication
B. Authorization
C. Accounting
D. Non-repudiation

Practice Question 1 Explanation

This is an example of a discretionary access control (DAC) system. The defining characteristic of a DAC system is that the owners of individual files can grant other users access to those files.

In a mandatory access control (MAC) system, file permissions are managed by the operating system and cannot be modified by individual users.

In a role-based access control (RBAC) system, users are assigned to roles based on their job responsibilities, and then permissions are granted to those roles.

In an attribute-based access control (ABAC) system, users are granted access to resources based on attributes assigned to their accounts. While ABAC is an incorrect answer choice used in this question, it is not specifically covered by the CC exam objectives.

Correct Answer: C. DAC

Practice Question 2 Explanation

This is a tricky question because the user is technically performing all of these actions. Before allowing a user to sign a contract, the system must be confident in their identity, and it gains this confidence through the authentication process. It must also be sure that the user is allowed to enter into the contract, which it does through the authorization process. And the lender will definitely want to keep a record of the action, which is done through the accounting process.

However, this question is about proving to a third party that the user signed the contract. This is preventing the user from denying the action and is a non-repudiation requirement.

Correct Answer: D. Non-repudiation

Domain 4:
Network Security

Network Security is the fourth domain of ISC2's Certified in Cybersecurity exam. It provides the knowledge that entry-level cybersecurity professionals need to know about securing computer networks. This domain includes the following three objectives:

4.1   Understand computer networking

4.2   Understand network threats and attacks

4.3   Understand network security infrastructure

Questions from this domain make up 24 percent of the questions on the CC exam, so you should expect to see 24 questions on your test covering the material in this part.

CHAPTER 13

Computer Networking
Objective 4.1 Understand Computer Networking

The computers that we use are powerful, but they become even more powerful when they're connected to each other. That's the role of a network: connecting computer systems together, whether it's within an office or to the global Internet. Networks allow us to send email messages around the world, stream video, print to a printer down the hall, and perform many other important tasks.

In this chapter, you'll learn about CC objective 4.1. The following subobjectives are covered in this chapter:

▶ **Networks (e.g., Open Systems Interconnection (OSI) model, Transmission Control Protocol/Internet Protocol (TCP/IP) model, Internet Protocol version 4 (IPv4), Internet Protocol version 6 (IPv6), WiFi)**
▶ **Ports**
▶ **Applications**

NETWORK TYPES

The networks in homes and offices are called *local area networks (LANs)*. LANs connect devices that are in the same building so that they can talk to each other and to servers, printers, and other devices located in the office.

LANs are then connected to *wide area networks (WANs)*. WANs connect offices in different locations and also connect users to the Internet. When a LAN is connected to a WAN, it allows users to become part of the global Internet and communicate with anyone they'd like.

Wi-Fi networks create powerful wireless LANs that allow users to use smartphones, laptops, and other networked devices anywhere in their home or office. I'll talk more about Wi-Fi networking later in this chapter.

You've probably also used a couple of other wireless networking technologies. *Bluetooth* networks are what are called *personal area networks (PANs)*. They're usually created by a computer or smartphone, and they're designed to support a single person. The main use of Bluetooth networks is to create wireless connections between a computer and its peripherals. Bluetooth allows users to use wireless headsets and connect their phones to their cars for hands-free access. The range of a Bluetooth network is around 30 feet, or 10 meters.

Near-field communication (NFC) technology allows extremely short-range wireless connections. In order for two devices to communicate using NFC, they need to be no more than a few centimeters apart. NFC technology is often used for wireless payments and building access control systems.

Bluetooth and NFC networks aren't general-purpose networks that connect many computers together, but they're very useful for short-range applications.

TCP/IP NETWORKING

Now that you understand a little about the types of network connections, let's talk about how data flows on a network. To do that, we need to dive into a suite of protocols that you've probably heard about but might not be familiar with: *TCP/IP*. You might have heard people refer to TCP/IP networking because it's the protocol that runs the Internet and basically every LAN on the planet.

The acronym TCP/IP has two parts. The first part is the *Transmission Control Protocol (TCP)*, and the second part is the *Internet Protocol (IP)*. Each of these protocols plays a vital role in making sure that data gets from point A to point B.

Internet Protocol

The first protocol in the TCP/IP suite is the Internet Protocol (IP). IP is responsible for routing information over the network. Even though it is referred to as the Internet Protocol, IP is used both on the Internet and on a LAN.

IP assigns each computer on the network its own address, called an *IP address*. I'll talk more about those addresses later in this chapter. For now, just know that IP addresses uniquely identify computers on a network and are the way that computers identify each other on an IP network.

When data travels on a TCP/IP network, the Internet Protocol breaks it up into small pieces called *packets*. Each packet is a few kilobytes of data. If you're sending a large file consisting of many megabytes or gigabytes, it will be divided up into thousands of smaller packets that are sent over the network.

The reason that data is broken into packets like this is to make networks more reliable. If you tried to stuff megabytes into a single transmission and that transmission failed for some reason, you'd have to do the whole thing over again. If you break that up into thousands of smaller packets and one of those packets fails, you only need to retransmit that single small packet.

Larger packets would also clog up networks. Think about a city street. When a lot of small cars are moving through the streets, traffic flows pretty smoothly. Now imagine a miles-long freight train trying to drive down a city street. That would clog up traffic for miles around, and nobody else would be able to use the road until the train left the city. That would leave a lot of unhappy computer users!

The Internet Protocol's job is to manage all of this work. You can just send a large file and IP will handle breaking it up into packets and then putting those packets back together again on the other side.

Transmission Control Protocol

The second protocol in the TCP/IP suite is the Transmission Control Protocol (TCP). TCP is responsible for setting up and tearing down connections between source and destination systems. TCP tracks the packets that are sent and controls the rate at which the packets are sent. If a packet is lost or damaged along the way, it's TCP's job to request that the sender transmit a new packet to replace the one that didn't arrive correctly. TCP is also responsible for correctly reordering the packets at their destination, confirming a reliable delivery.

User Datagram Protocol

The *User Datagram Protocol* (UDP) is an alternative to TCP. It has less overhead but does not guarantee the delivery of packets from one system to another. UDP lacks the reliability of TCP, but it operates much faster than TCP. UDP is commonly used in situations where speed is more important than ensuring that every single packet reaches its destination. Streaming video is one example of an application where UDP is well suited.

Internet Control Message Protocol

The *Internet Control Message Protocol (ICMP)* is the housekeeping protocol of the Internet. It is part of the TCP/IP suite, and it's designed to allow networked devices and systems to communicate with each other about the operation of the network. For example, ICMP can be used to detect whether remote systems are live on the network, to discover the network path between two systems, and to report issues with network devices.

A lot of other stuff is involved in getting TCP/IP up and running on a network, but fortunately you won't need to know about that for the CC exam.

OSI Model

Network models describe how all of these protocols fit together. The most common of these is the *Open Systems Interconnection (OSI) model*.

The OSI model describes networks as having seven different layers, as shown in Figure 13.1.

▶ The first layer, the *Physical layer*, is responsible for sending bits over the network using wires, radio waves, fiber optics, and other means.

▶ The second layer, the *Data-Link layer*, transfers data between two nodes connected to the same physical network.

▶ The third layer, the *Network layer*, expands networks to many different nodes. The Internet Protocol works at this layer.

▶ The fourth layer, the *Transport layer*, creates connections between systems and transfers data in a reliable manner. TCP and UDP are transport layer protocols.

▶ The fifth layer, the *Session layer*, manages the exchange of communications between systems.

▶ The sixth layer, the *Presentation layer*, translates data so that it can be transmitted on a network. This layer determines how to represent a character in terms of bits and performs encryption and decryption.

▶ The seventh layer, the *Application layer*, determines how users interact with the data, using web browsers and other client applications. Protocols like HTTP, SMTP, and SSH exist at the Application layer.

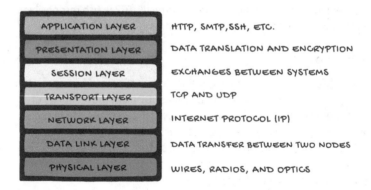

FIGURE 13.1 The Open Systems Interconnection (OSI) network model

IP ADDRESSING

Just like telephones use phone numbers and postal mail uses street addresses, the Internet needs an addressing scheme to ensure that data reaches its intended destination. The addresses that are used by the Internet Protocol are known as *IP addresses*.

In most cases, IP addresses are written in what's known as the dotted quad notation of IPv4. This means that they are four numbers, separated by periods. Each number can range between 0 and 255. For example, you might have a computer that uses the IP address 10.15.100.240.

> **NOTE**
>
> The dotted quad notation is used by IPv4, the most common protocol in use today. IPv6, the next generation of addresses, uses eight groups of four hexadecimal digits. For example, fae0:2660:a0a1:2efe:c84b:4c44:3467:a1ed is an IPv6 address.

A system's IP address uniquely identifies it on a network. If the system is directly connected to the Internet, the IP address it uses must not be used by any other system in the world, just as your mobile phone number is not used elsewhere in the world.

Systems that are connected to private networks, such as the one in your home or office, may use private IP addresses that are reusable on other networks. Your router or firewall takes care of translating those addresses to public IP addresses when you communicate over the Internet.

The following two IP addresses are involved in every network communication:

► The *source address* indicates the system sending information.
► The *destination address* indicates the system receiving information.

As two systems communicate back and forth, the source and destination addresses will swap places, depending on who sends each packet. For example, imagine the communication between a user with IP address 10.12.0.1 and a web server with IP address 10.51.1.2. When the user is sending data to the web server, the source address is the user's IP address, and the destination server is the web server's IP address, as shown in Figure 13.2.

10.12.0.1   10.51.1.2

SOURCE: 10.12.0.1
DESTINATION: 10.51.1.2

FIGURE 13.2 Communication from a user to a web server

When the web server replies and sends data back to the user, the direction switches; the web server's IP address is the source address and the user's IP address becomes the destination address, as shown in Figure 13.3.

IP addresses can be assigned in two ways:

► You can assign an IP address *statically*. This means that you go into the system's settings and manually specify its IP address. You are responsible for ensuring that you choose a unique address that fits within the range for that network.
► You can assign an IP address *dynamically* by using the *Dynamic Host Configuration Protocol (DHCP)*. DHCP allows you to configure a pool of IP addresses,

and then DHCP will automatically assign those addresses to systems as they join the network. Typically, servers are configured with static IP addresses, and end-user devices are configured with dynamically changing IP addresses.

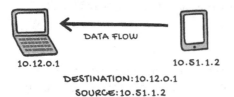

FIGURE 13.3 Communication from a web server to a user

If a system is not configured with a static IP address, it reaches out on the network searching for a DHCP server that can supply it with a dynamic address. If the system is unable to find a DHCP server, it assigns itself an address using *Automatic Private IP Addressing (APIPA)*. APIPA addresses all begin with 169.254. If you see one of these addresses in use on your network, it means that something has likely gone wrong, as the system with that address was unable to obtain a valid IP address. In all but the smallest networks, addresses should be assigned by a DHCP server instead of being left to APIPA to assign.

Identifying Valid IPv4 Addresses

One of the things that you may be asked to do on the exam is to identify which IP addresses are valid for a host on a network. If you see a question like this, you should approach it using the process of elimination. The following are a few simple rules that you can follow to eliminate invalid IP addresses:

No octet in an IP address should ever be larger than 255.   If you see a number greater than 255 in an IP address, that is not a valid address and you can immediately eliminate it as a possibility.

IP addresses starting with the number 127 are reserved for use as loopback addresses.   These addresses always reference the local system and are not valid as addresses on a network. The most common loopback address is 127.0.0.1, and when it's used in communications, it's the equivalent of telling a system to talk to itself. You should never see an address beginning with 127 as a host address for this reason.

The first number in an IP address should never be higher than 223.   While you can have values up to 255 in any octet, numbers higher than 223 in the first octet are reserved for special uses and shouldn't be assigned to systems. Addresses with first numbers between 224 and 239 are called *multicast addresses*. They are used for sending messages to many systems at the same time and should never be assigned to an individual system. Addresses beginning with values between 240 and 255 are reserved for experimental use and, again, should not be found on individual systems.

Domain Name System

Computers use IP addresses to communicate over the network but those addresses are very difficult for people to remember. Just imagine if you had to memorize the IP address of every web server that you needed to access! The *Domain Name System (DNS)* allows people to use easily recognizable names in place of IP addresses.

DNS servers translate the names that you're more familiar with, such as `www.certmike.com`, into the IP addresses that computers use to communicate, such as `54.174.107.98`. DNS is responsible for translating the *uniform resource locator (URL)* addresses that are commonly used for websites into the IP addresses associated with the servers supporting those sites.

NOTE

All of this terminology might be a little confusing. A domain name is a top-level name that may be registered by a company, organization, or individual. For example, `certmike.com` and `comptia.org` are both domain names. A URL is the address of a specific web page or other resource hosted on that domain. For example, `www.certmike.com/cc/` is a URL.

Every time you connect to a network, that network provides your computer with the IP address of a local *DNS server* that it can use to look up IP addresses. Then, whenever you type in the domain name of a website in your browser, your computer sends a request to the local DNS server asking it for the IP address associated with that name.

If the server knows the answer to your question, it simply responds to the request with the IP address, and then your web browser can go ahead and connect to the website using its IP address. If the local DNS server doesn't know the answer to your question, it contacts other DNS servers to determine the correct answer and then responds to you.

DNS is a hierarchical system, and organizations who own domain names designate DNS servers that are the responsible sources of information about their domain name. When a local DNS server needs to perform a lookup, it asks a series of questions that eventually lead it to the definitive answer from the DNS server that is responsible for a domain.

NETWORK PORTS AND APPLICATIONS

IP addresses can uniquely identify each system on a network, but those systems might be responsible for running many different applications. That's where network ports come into play.

Network ports are particular locations on a system associated with a specific application. Imagine that each computer on the network is an apartment building and each application is an individual apartment. The IP address on the computer is like the street address on the apartment building, but once you arrive at the building, you need specific instructions to get to the right apartment. The network port is like the apartment number, guiding traffic to the correct application.

Network ports are represented using a number ranging from 0 to 65,535. Different ranges of ports are used in different ways.

- ▶ Ports between 0 and 1,023 are called *well-known ports*. These are reserved for common applications and assigned by Internet authorities. Using well-known ports ensures that everyone on the Internet will know how to find common services on a system, such as web servers, email servers, and other commonly used applications. For example, web servers use the well-known port 80, whereas secure web servers use port 443 by default.
- ▶ Ports between 1,024 and 49,151 are known as *registered ports*. Application vendors can register their applications to use these ports. For example, Microsoft reserved port 1433 for SQL Server database connections, while Oracle registered port 1521 for its own database's use.
- ▶ Ports above 49,151 are set aside as *dynamic ports* that applications can use on a temporary basis.

One of the burdensome tasks on any cybersecurity exam is that you must memorize some important facts. Common port numbers are one of those memorization tasks; indeed, it's quite helpful to have these committed to memory when you're working as a cybersecurity professional. Table 13.1 shows some common ports that you should know as you prepare for the CC exam.

TABLE 13.1 Common TCP Ports

Port	Service
53	DNS
20/21	FTP
80	HTTP (unencrypted)
443	HTTPS (encrypted)

Port	Service
1433	Microsoft SQL Server Databases
1521	Oracle Databases
3389	RDP
25	SMTP (unencrypted)
587	SMTP (encrypted)
22	SSH

SECURING WI-FI NETWORKS

One of the major responsibilities of IT professionals is to secure wireless networks to protect the traffic they carry from eavesdropping attacks and to protect the network from unauthorized access. There are a few best practices you can follow to protect your wireless network.

Disable SSID Broadcasting

Each wireless network has a name that identifies it to users. This name is what you see on your phone or laptop when you're choosing the network you'd like to use. The technical term for this name is the *service set identifier (SSID)*. By default, wireless networks advertise themselves to potential users by broadcasting their SSID, telling everyone in the local area that the network is available and accepting connections. If you don't want to advertise your network, you can disable SSID broadcasting, hiding the network from users who don't already know that it is there. Figure 13.4 shows how macOS displays the SSIDs that are broadcast in an area.

Change Default Passwords

Your wireless access point also has an administrative password that allows you to connect to the device and configure the wireless network and its security settings. The access point may have come from the manufacturer with a default password already set. It is printed in the user manual or on a label on the device itself. You should, as a matter of habit, immediately change these default passwords to strong passwords known only to you and other network administrators.

FIGURE 13.4 **SSIDs appearing on a macOS system**

Authenticate Wi-Fi Users

You'll also need to decide which type of wireless network you'd like to run. Open networks are available to anyone who comes across them and would like to use them. Other networks use some type of authentication to limit access.

Preshared Keys

Preshared keys (PSK) are the simplest kind of wireless authentication and are commonly used on home Wi-Fi networks. In the preshared key approach, the network uses an encryption key to control access. Whenever a user wants to connect a device to the network, they must enter the preshared key on the device. If you've ever been at an office or public place where there's a Wi-Fi password posted on the wall, that's an example of a preshared key.

Preshared keys work fine, but they have major limitations that prevent them from being used on large networks:

▶ Changing the network encryption key is a tremendous burden. Each time the key changes, users must reconfigure all wireless devices to use the new key. This might not be bad on a home network supporting a handful of users, but it is impractical in most business environments.

▶ The use of a shared key prevents the identification of individual users and the restriction of access by user identity. For example, if a user leaves the organization, network administrators have no way to revoke that user's wireless network access short of changing the preshared key on all wireless devices in the organization.

Enterprise Authentication

The more common way to approach wireless authentication is through the use of *enterprise authentication*. In this approach, the organization runs an authentication server that verifies user credentials and ensures that only authorized users access the network. In this approach, instead of entering a preshared key, users enter their individual username and password or provide other credentials to access the network.

Captive Portals

The third approach to wireless authentication is with the use of *captive portals*, such as the one shown in Figure 13.5. You might not be familiar with the term captive portal, but you've certainly seen them in use in hotels, airports, coffee shops, and other public locations. Captive portals provide authentication on unencrypted wireless networks. When a user connects to a network using a captive portal, they are redirected to a web page that requires them to authenticate before gaining access to the network. This authentication may be as simple as accepting the terms of service, or it may require an account password or even a credit card payment to escape the captive portal and use the Internet.

Wireless Encryption

Network administrators can choose to add encryption to wireless networks to protect communications against eavesdropping. Wireless encryption is a best practice for network security. Encryption hides the true content of network traffic from people without the decryption key. It takes an insecure communications technology—radio waves—and makes it secure.

Wired Equivalent Privacy

The original approach to solving this problem was a technology known as *Wired Equivalent Privacy (WEP)*. WEP was used for a long time but is now known to suffer from some very serious security vulnerabilities. These issues are so significant that security professionals no longer consider WEP secure, so it should never be used on a modern network.

FIGURE 13.5 **A captive portal used for wireless authentication**

Wi-Fi Protected Access

A newer technology called Wi-Fi Protected Access, or WPA, replaced WEP all the way back in 2003. This first version, just called WPA, used the *Temporal Key Integrity Protocol (TKIP)* to add security that WEP didn't have. TKIP changes the encryption key for each packet, preventing an attacker from discovering the key after monitoring the network for a long period of time.

However, as happens with many security technologies, vulnerabilities in WPA have now come to light that also make it a poor choice for use on wireless networks.

Wi-Fi Protected Access v2

In 2004, *WPA2* was released as an upgrade to WPA. Instead of simply trying to add security onto the old WEP standard, WPA2 uses an encryption protocol that is based on the *Advanced Encryption Standard (AES)*. It has a really long name, Counter Mode Cipher Block Chaining Message Authentication Code Protocol, but you just need to know it as *CCMP*.

Security researchers have discovered some potential issues with WPA2, but it is still considered secure and is widely used.

Wi-Fi Protected Access v3

As of 2020, new wireless devices are required to support the *WPA3* standard. WPA3 also supports the CCMP protocol, but it adds a new technology called *Simultaneous*

Authentication of Equals (SAE). SAE is a secure key exchange protocol that provides a more secure initial setup of encrypted wireless communications.

> **EXAM TIP**
>
> To help you prepare for the CC exam, Figure 13.6 summarizes all of this wireless encryption with a quick reference table.

STANDARD	SECURITY STATUS
OPEN NETWORK	INSECURE
WEP	INSECURE
WPA	INSECURE
WPA2	SECURE
WPA3	SECURE

FIGURE 13.6 Wireless encryption summary

EXAM ESSENTIALS

▶ The Open Systems Interconnection (OSI) model describes network communications using seven layers. They are, in order, the Physical layer, Data-Link layer, Network layer, Transport layer, Session layer, Presentation layer, and Application layer.

▶ Modern networking uses a suite of protocols called TCP/IP. This suite uses the Internet Protocol (IP) for routing information over networks at the Network layer. Each communication also uses a Transport layer protocol, which is commonly the Transmission Control Protocol (TCP) or the User Datagram Protocol (UDP).

▶ A system's IP address uniquely identifies it on a network. IPv4 addresses use the dotted quad notation of four integers ranging from 0 to 255 separated by periods. IPv6 addresses use eight groups of four hexadecimal digits separated by colons.

▶ Network ports are particular logical locations on a system associated with specific applications. Port numbers range from 0 to 65,535.

▶ Wi-Fi networks use a variety of authentication technologies, including preshared keys, enterprise authentication, and captive portals. In addition, Wi-Fi networks should use either WPA2 or WPA3 encryption to provide secure communications.

Practice Question 1

You are assigning a host address to a new system on a network using a static IP address assignment. Which one of the following is a valid IP address?

A. 12.274.16.4
B. 127.19.6.200
C. 194.243.129.144
D. 240.1.15.2

Practice Question 2

Tom is configuring a Wi-Fi network for a user who will be working from home. He would like to configure the network so that it is as strongly protected from eavesdropping as possible. Which encryption standard should Tom use?

A. WEP
B. WPA2
C. WPA3
D. WPA4

Practice Question 1 Explanation

You can walk through the three rules of valid IP addresses and answer this question by the process of elimination. If you rule out any invalid IP addresses, you are left with the one valid address. First, no value in an IP address should ever be higher than 255. That eliminates the first option because it contains the value 274.

Second, the first value in a host address should never be 127. That eliminates the second option.

And, finally, the first value in a host address should never be higher than 223. That eliminates the last option, which contains 240 as an octet value. That leaves one valid address: 194.243.129.144.

You should be prepared to answer questions like this one when you take the CC exam. If you see a question like this, be sure to read it carefully. Depending on how the question is phrased, it might be asking you to identify which one of a set of addresses is valid or which one of a set of addresses is invalid. Don't get tricked by assuming what the question is asking before you read the entire question.

Correct Answer: C. 194.243.129.144

Practice Question 2 Explanation

Tom should use the WPA3 standard because it is the strongest available Wi-Fi encryption technology.

The WPA2 protocol is also acceptable for use on modern networks, but it is not as strong as the WPA3 protocol, making WPA3 a better choice.

The WEP protocol is an outdated protocol that is no longer considered secure and should not be used.

The WPA4 protocol does not yet exist.

Correct Answer: C. WPA3

CHAPTER 14

Network Threats and Attacks

Objective 4.2 Understand Network Threats and Attacks

Understanding cybersecurity involves recognizing the various threats that can compromise data and systems. This chapter serves as a guide for both security professionals and general users to learn about different types of network-based threats and how they operate.

In this chapter, you'll learn about the first subobjective of CC objective 4.2. The remaining material for this objective is covered in Chapter 15, "Threat Identification and Protection." The following subobjective is covered in this chapter:

▶ **Types of threats (e.g., distributed denial-of-service (DDoS), virus, worm, Trojan, man-in-the-middle (MITM), side-channel)**

MALWARE

Malware (or malicious software) is one of the most significant threats to computer security. Malware objects infect computer systems and then perform some type of evil action: possibly stealing information, damaging data, or otherwise disrupting normal use of the system. As a security professional, you need to understand the various types of malicious code and how they work to infect systems.

Every piece of malware that you encounter will have two components: a propagation mechanism and a payload. The *propagation mechanism* is how the malware spreads from one system to another. Propagation mechanisms vary between malware types.

The *payload* is the malicious action that the malware performs. Any type of malware object can carry any type of payload. For example, a malware payload might search your hard drive for credit card statements and tax returns, encrypt data and make it unavailable until you pay a ransom, or monitor your keystrokes until you log in to your bank account, compromising your username and password.

Viruses

The first type of malware that we need to talk about is the *virus*. Most computer users are already familiar with the concept of viruses, but they often misapply the term to any type of malware. Computer viruses take their name from biological viruses.

The defining characteristic of a virus is that it spreads from system to system based on some type of user action. This might be opening an email attachment, clicking a link to a malicious website, or inserting an infected USB drive into a system. Viruses don't spread unless someone triggers or activates them. Therefore, one of the best ways to protect against viruses is through user education.

Worms

The second type of malware is the *worm*. Worms spread from system to system without user interaction. They spread under their own power. Worms reach out and exploit system vulnerabilities, infecting systems without the user doing anything. Once a worm has infected a system, it uses that system as a new base for spreading to other parts of the local area network or the broader Internet.

Worms require vulnerable systems to spread. Therefore, the best way to defend against worms is keeping systems updated with the most recent operating system and application patches.

Trojan Horses

The final type of malware to discuss is the *Trojan horse*. You may already know the story of the Trojan horse from the 12th century B.C. The Greek army, which had laid siege to the city of Troy for 10 years, built a gigantic wooden horse and hid soldiers inside of it. The rest of the army then pretended to sail away, leaving the horse for the Trojans to claim as a trophy. The Trojans opened their city walls and brought the horse inside. That night, the Greek army poured out of the horse and destroyed the city.

In the world of malware, Trojan horses work in a similar way. They pretend to be legitimate pieces of software that a user might want to download and install. When the user runs the program, it does perform as expected; however, the Trojan horse also carries a malicious hidden payload that performs some unwanted action behind the scenes. Since Trojan horses arrive on systems when users install software, application control provides a good defense against this threat. Application control solutions limit the software that can run on systems to titles and versions specifically approved by administrators.

EXAM TIP

Different malware objects spread in different ways. Viruses spread between systems after a user action; worms spread under their own power; and Trojan horses pose as beneficial software with a hidden malicious effect. As you prepare for the CC exam, you'll want to remember the differences between these objects.

EAVESDROPPING ATTACKS

In some cases, an attacker can gain physical or logical access to the network and *eavesdrop* on communications between two systems. These attacks can be especially dangerous because they allow the attacker to potentially decrypt encrypted communications and view confidential information without the sender's knowledge or consent.

All eavesdropping attacks require some compromise of the communications path between a client and a server. This might include tapping into a network device or cable or conducting a specialized attack to trick a system into sending traffic directly to an attacker instead of the intended recipient.

On-Path Attacks

On-path attacks take eavesdropping to the next level by inserting an attacker in between the client and the server. This section discusses two types of on-path attacks: man-in-the-middle (MitM) and man-in-the-browser (MitB) attacks.

Figure 14.1 shows how most people imagine web communication takes place. The user, running a web browser, initiates a connection to a server located somewhere off in a data center.

USER   SERVER

FIGURE 14.1 The common perception of web communication

The reality is that those communications travel over many network connections along the way, as shown in Figure 14.2. Any one of the devices in the middle represents a possible point where an eavesdropper might listen in on the communication. Encryption, such as that used with HTTPS, prevents any of those intermediate devices from viewing or altering the communication.

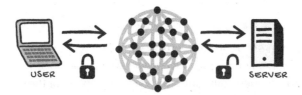

FIGURE 14.2 **The actual network path for web communication**

Man-in-the-Middle Attacks

Since simple eavesdropping is easily defeated by encryption, attackers can use a *man-in-the-middle attack* to step up the game a bit. In this attack, the attacker tricks the sending system during the initial communication. This might be done by reconfiguring a network device or by using DNS or ARP poisoning.

Instead of establishing communications with a legitimate server, the user connects directly to the attacker, as shown in Figure 14.3. The attacker, in turn, connects to the legitimate server. The user authenticates to the fake server set up by the attacker, and the attacker acts as a relay—the man in the middle—and can view all of the communications that take place between the client and the server. The attacker receives the requests from the user, passes them onto the server, receives the real responses, reads them, and then replays them to the original user, who has no idea that there is a man in the middle intercepting those communications.

FIGURE 14.3 **A man-in-the-middle (MitM) attack**

Man-in-the-Browser Attacks

The *man-in-the-browser attack* is a variation on the man-in-the-middle attack, where the attacker compromises the user's web browser or a browser plugin or extension to gain access to web communications. The major difference is that the attacker isn't present on a different network device from the user and server. The attacker is actually present on the user's computer.

DENIAL-OF-SERVICE ATTACKS

Most of the attack techniques used by hackers focus on undermining the confidentiality or integrity of data. By far, the most common motivation of an attacker is to steal sensitive information, such as credit card numbers or Social Security numbers, or to alter information in an unauthorized fashion, such as increasing bank account balances or defacing a website.

Some attacks, however, focus on disrupting the legitimate use of a system. Unlike other attacks, these target the availability leg of the CIA triad. These attacks are known as *denial-of-service (DoS)* attacks.

A DoS attack, as shown in Figure 14.4, is an attack that makes a system or resource unavailable to legitimate users. It sends thousands or millions of requests to a network, server, or application, overwhelming it and making it unable to answer any requests. Done well, it is very difficult to distinguish DoS attack requests from legitimate traffic.

FIGURE 14.4 A denial-of-service (DoS) attack

There are two huge issues with this basic denial-of-service approach from the attacker's perspective:

▶ They require large amounts of bandwidth. Sending a lot of requests that tie up the server requires a large network connection. It becomes a case of who has the bigger network connection.
▶ They are easy to block. Once the victim recognizes they are under attack, they can simply block the IP addresses of the attackers.

That's where *distributed denial-of-service (DDoS)* attacks come into play. They use botnets consisting of thousands of compromised systems located all over the globe to overwhelm their target with traffic, as shown in Figure 14.5. The attack requests come from all over the place, so it is difficult to distinguish them from legitimate requests.

DoS and DDoS attacks are serious threats to system administrators because they can quickly overwhelm a network with illegitimate traffic. Defending against them requires that security professionals understand them well and implement blocking technology on the network that identifies and weeds out suspected attack traffic before it reaches servers. This is often done with the cooperation of Internet service providers and third-party DDoS protection services.

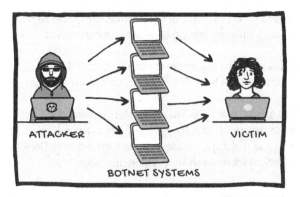

FIGURE 14.5 A distributed denial-of-service (DDoS) attack

SIDE-CHANNEL ATTACKS

Computer systems generate characteristic footprints of activity, such as changes in processor utilization, power consumption, or electromagnetic radiation. *Side-channel attacks* seek to use this information to monitor system activity and retrieve information that is actively being used.

For example, if a cryptographic system is improperly implemented, it may be possible to capture the electromagnetic radiation emanating from that system and use the collected signal to determine the plaintext information that was being encrypted.

Timing attacks are an example of a side-channel attack where the attacker measures precisely how long cryptographic operations take to complete, gaining information about the cryptographic process that may be used to undermine its security.

EXAM ESSENTIALS

▶ Different malware objects spread in different ways. Viruses spread between systems after a user action; worms spread under their own power; and Trojan horses pose as beneficial software with a hidden malicious effect.

▶ In a man-in-the-middle (MitM) attack , the attacker tricks the sending system into communicating with the attacker, rather than the intended server. The user authenticates to the fake server set up by the attacker, and the attacker acts as a relay and can view all of the communications that take place between the client and the server.

▶ Denial-of-service (DoS) attacks send unwanted traffic from a single attacker system to a victim server, overwhelming it with requests. Distributed denial-of-service (DDoS) attacks use a botnet to send the traffic from many different sources.

Practice Question 1

Kim is the system administrator for a small business network that is experiencing security problems. She is in the office one evening working on the problem, and nobody else is there. As she is watching, she can see that systems on the other side of the office that were previously behaving normally are now exhibiting signs of infection one after the other. Which type of malware is Kim likely dealing with?

A. Virus
B. Worm
C. Trojan horse
D. Logic bomb

Practice Question 2

Which one of the following statements about denial-of-service (DoS) attacks is incorrect?

A. They originate from many different sources.
B. They can disrupt the availability of systems.
C. They require large amounts of bandwidth.
D. They are easily detectible.

Practice Question 1 Explanation

Worms have built-in propagation mechanisms that do not require user interaction, such as scanning for systems containing known vulnerabilities and then exploiting those vulnerabilities to gain access.

Viruses and Trojan horses typically require user interaction to spread. Nobody else is in the office and the malware is still spreading, so it is unlikely to be this type of traffic.

Logic bombs do not spread from system to system but lie in wait until certain conditions are met, triggering the delivery of their payload.

Correct Answer: B. Worm

Practice Question 2 Explanation

Standard denial-of-service (DoS) attacks do not originate from many different sources; they originate from a single source. Distributed denial-of-service (DDoS) attacks originate from many different sources.

DoS attacks can disrupt the availability of systems. They do require large amounts of bandwidth, and, because they originate from a single source, they are easily detectible.

Correct Answer: A. They originate from many different sources.

CHAPTER 15

Threat Identification and Prevention

Objective 4.2 Understand Network Threats and Attacks

Understanding and mitigating network threats is critical in safeguarding data and systems. Intrusion detection systems, intrusion prevention systems, firewalls, and antivirus software play pivotal roles in identifying and neutralizing potential attacks. Additionally, vulnerability scanning ensures that security weaknesses are promptly identified and addressed, contributing to a comprehensive network security strategy.

In this chapter, you'll learn about the second and third subobjectives of CC objective 4.2. The remaining material for this objective is covered in Chapter 14, "Network Threats and Attacks." The following subobjectives are covered in this chapter:

▶ Identification (e.g., intrusion detection system (IDS), host-based intrusion detection system (HIDS), network intrusion detection system (NIDS))
▶ Prevention (e.g., antivirus, scans, firewalls, intrusion prevention system (IPS))

ANTIVIRUS SOFTWARE

As you learned in Chapter 14, malware is one of the most common threats to the security of computers and mobile devices, and you can use a set of tools to protect against these threats. Modern *antivirus software* protects against viruses, worms, Trojan horses, and other types of malicious code. Antivirus software uses two different mechanisms to protect systems against malicious software:

▶ *Signature detection* uses databases of known malware patterns and scans the files and memory of a system for any data matching the pattern of known malicious software. If signature detection finds suspect content, it can remove it from the system or quarantine it for further analysis. When you're using signature detection, it is critical that you frequently update the virus definition file to ensure that you have current signatures for newly discovered malware.

▶ *Behavior detection* takes a different approach. Instead of using patterns of known malicious activity, these systems attempt to model normal activity and then report when they discover anomalies—activity that deviates from that normal pattern.

Behavioral detection techniques are found in advanced malware protection tools known as *endpoint detection and response (EDR)* solutions. These advanced tools go beyond basic signature detection and perform deep instrumentation of endpoints. They analyze memory and processor usage, registry entries, network communications, and other system behavior characteristics. They offer advanced real-time protection against malware and other security threats by using agents installed on endpoint devices to watch for signs of malicious activity and trigger automated responses to defend systems from attack.

In addition, they often have the capability of performing *sandboxing*. When a system receives a suspicious executable, the advanced malware protection system sends that executable to a malware sandbox before allowing it to run on the protected system. In that sandbox, the malware protection solution runs the executable and watches its behavior, checking for suspicious activities. If the malware behaves in a manner that resembles an attack, it is not allowed to execute on the protected endpoint.

INTRUSION DETECTION AND PREVENTION

Intrusion detection systems (IDS) and *intrusion prevention systems (IPS)* play an extremely important role in the defense of networks against hackers and other security threats.

Intrusion Detection

Intrusion detection systems sit on the network and monitor traffic, searching for signs of potentially malicious traffic. For example, an IDS might notice that a request bound for a web server contains a SQL injection attack, a malformed packet is attempting to create a denial of service, a user's login attempt seems unusual based on the time of day and prior patterns, or that a system on the internal network is attempting to contact a botnet command and control server.

All of these situations are examples of security issues that administrators would obviously want to know about. Intrusion detection systems identify these types of situations and then alert administrators to the issue for further investigation.

Intrusion Prevention

In many cases, administrators are not available to immediately review alerts and take action or are simply overwhelmed by the sheer volume of alerts generated by an IDS.

That's where intrusion prevention comes into play. Intrusion prevention systems are just like intrusion detection systems but with a twist: They can take immediate corrective action in response to a detected threat. In most cases, this means blocking the potentially malicious traffic from entering the network.

Environments Monitored

IDS and IPS systems can monitor two different types of environments:

▶ *Host-based IDS (HIDS)* and *host-based IPS (HIPS)* systems monitor and protect individual devices like computers and servers. They analyze the system's files and operations to detect suspicious activities or unauthorized changes.

▶ *Network-based IDS (NIDS)* and *network-based IPS (NIPS)* systems focus on safeguarding the entire network. They monitor network traffic and analyze packets to detect and prevent malicious activities or intrusions that could harm the network as a whole.

Classification Errors

Intrusion detection systems can make mistakes. Two types of classification errors are caused by these systems, and monitoring those errors is an important part of security analytics.

▶ *False positive errors* occur when the system alerts administrators to an attack but the attack does not actually exist. This is an annoyance to the administrator, who wastes time investigating the alert, and may lead to administrators ignoring future alerts.

▶ *False negative errors* occur when an attack actually takes place but the IDS does not notice it.

Detection Techniques

Intrusion detection and prevention systems use two different techniques to identify suspicious traffic: signature detection and anomaly detection.

Signature Detection

The most common, and most effective, method is called *signature detection*. Signature-based detection systems contain very large databases that have patterns of data (or signatures) known to be associated with malicious activity. When the system spots network traffic matching one of those signatures, it triggers an intrusion alert.

The downside to this approach is that a signature-based system cannot detect a previously unknown attack. If you're one of the first victims of a new attack, it will sneak right past a signature detection system. The upside is that if the signatures are well designed, these systems work very well with a low false positive rate. Signature detection is reliable, time-tested technology.

Anomaly Detection

The second method is known as *anomaly detection*. This model takes a completely different approach to the intrusion detection problem. Instead of trying to develop signatures for all possible malicious activity, the anomaly detection system tries to develop a model of normal activity and then report deviations from that model as suspicious.

For example, an anomaly detection system might notice that a user who normally connects to the VPN from home during the early evening hours is suddenly connecting from Asia in the middle of the night. The system can then either alert administrators or block the connection, depending on the policy.

Anomaly detection does have the potential to notice new attack types, but it has a high false positive error rate and is not widely used by security administrators.

FIREWALLS

Network *firewalls* serve as the security guards of a network, analyzing all attempts to connect to systems on a network and determining whether the request should be allowed or denied according to the organization's security policy. They also play an important role in network segmentation.

Firewalls often sit at the network perimeter, in between an organization's routers and the Internet. From this network location, they can easily see all inbound and outbound connections. Traffic on the internal network can flow between trusted systems unimpeded, but anything crossing the perimeter to or from the Internet must be evaluated by the firewall.

Typical border firewalls have three network interfaces because they connect three different security zones together, as shown in Figure 15.1.

One interface connects to the Internet or another untrusted network. This is the interface between the protected networks and the outside world. Generally speaking, firewalls allow many different kinds of connections out to this network when initiated by a system on more trusted networks, but they block most inbound connection attempts, allowing only those that meet the organization's security policy.

A second interface connects to the organization's *intranet*. This is the internal network where most systems reside. This intranet zone can be further subdivided into segments for endpoint systems, wireless networks, guest networks, data center networks, and other business needs. The firewall can be configured to control access between those subnets, or the organization can use additional firewalls to segment those networks.

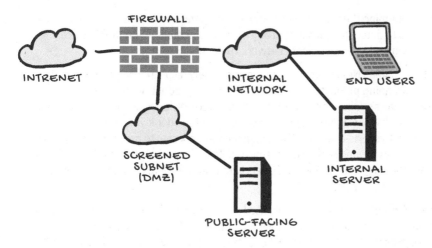

FIGURE 15.1 Network firewalls divide networks into three zones

The third interface connects to the *screened subnet*. Also known as the DMZ, the screened subnet is a network where you can place systems that must accept connections from the outside world, such as a mail or web server. Those systems are placed in a separate security zone because they have a higher risk of compromise. If an attacker compromises a DMZ system, the firewall still blocks them from breaching the intranet.

VULNERABILITY SCANNING

Technical environments are complex. They include servers, endpoint systems, network devices, and many other components that each run millions of lines of code and process complex configurations. No matter how much you work to secure these systems, they will inevitably contain vulnerabilities, and new vulnerabilities will arise on a regular basis.

Vulnerability management programs play a crucial role in identifying, prioritizing, and remediating vulnerabilities in technical environments. They use *vulnerability scanning* to detect new vulnerabilities as they arise and then implement a remediation workflow that addresses the highest-priority vulnerabilities. Every organization should incorporate vulnerability management into their cybersecurity program.

As you fill out your cybersecurity toolkit, you will want to have a network vulnerability scanner, an application scanner, and a web application scanner. Vulnerability scanners are often leveraged for preventive scanning and testing and are also found in penetration testers' toolkits, where they help identify systems that testers can exploit. This fact also means they're a favorite tool of attackers!

Network Vulnerability Scanning

Network vulnerability scanners are capable of probing a wide range of network-connected devices for known vulnerabilities. They reach out to any systems connected to the network, attempt to determine the type of device and its configuration, and then launch targeted tests designed to detect the presence of any known vulnerabilities on those devices.

The following tools are examples of network vulnerability scanners:

▶ Tenable's Nessus is a well-known and widely respected network vulnerability scanning product. It was one of the earliest products in this field.

▶ Qualys's vulnerability scanner is a more recently developed commercial network vulnerability scanner that offers a unique deployment model using a software-as-a-service (SaaS) management console to run scans using appliances located both in on-premises data centers and in the cloud.

▶ The open source OpenVAS offers a free alternative to commercial vulnerability scanners.

These are three of the most commonly used network vulnerability scanners. Many other products are on the market today, and every mature organization should have at least one scanner in its toolkit. Many organizations choose to deploy two different vulnerability scanning products in the same environment as a defense-in-depth control.

Application Scanning

Application scanning tools are commonly used as part of the software development process. These tools analyze custom-developed software to identify common security vulnerabilities. Application testing occurs using the following three software testing techniques:

▶ *Static testing* analyzes code without executing it. This approach points developers directly to vulnerabilities and often provides specific remediation suggestions.

▶ *Dynamic testing* executes code as part of the test, running all the interfaces that the code exposes to the user with a variety of inputs, searching for vulnerabilities.

▶ *Interactive testing* combines static and dynamic testing, analyzing the source code while testers interact with the application through exposed interfaces.

Application testing should be an integral part of the software development process. Many organizations introduce testing requirements into the software release process, requiring that any code released into production have a test that shows no significant vulnerabilities.

Web Application Scanning

Web application scanners are specialized tools used to examine the security of web applications. These tools test for web-specific vulnerabilities, such as SQL injection, cross-site scripting (XSS), and cross-site request forgery (CSRF) vulnerabilities. They work by combining traditional network scans of web servers with detailed probing of web applications, using such techniques as sending known malicious input sequences in attempts to break the application.

EXAM ESSENTIALS

▶ Intrusion detection systems monitor an environment for signs of malicious activity and report that activity to administrators. Intrusion prevention systems go a step further and attempt to actually block the activity.

▶ Host-based intrusion detection and prevention systems monitor and protect individual devices like computers and servers. They analyze the system's files and operations to detect suspicious activities or unauthorized changes.

▶ Network-based intrusion detection and prevention systems focus on safeguarding the entire network. They monitor network traffic and analyze packets to detect and prevent malicious activities or intrusions that could harm the network as a whole.

▶ Network firewalls serve as the security guards of a network, analyzing all attempts to connect to systems on a network and determining whether the request should be allowed or denied according to the organization's security policy.

Practice Question 1

Tara recently analyzed the results of a vulnerability scan report and found that a vulnerability reported by the scanner did not exist because the system was actually patched as specified. Which type of error occurred?

A. False positive
B. False negative
C. True positive
D. True negative

Practice Question 2

Valerie recently installed a new device on her network that monitors traffic that passes through the organization's firewall and blocks any traffic that appears to contain malicious attacks. Which type of system has she installed?

A. HIPS
B. HIDS
C. NIPS
D. NIDS

Practice Question 1 Explanation

A false positive error occurs when the vulnerability scanner reports a vulnerability that does not actually exist. That is the case in this scenario.

A false negative error occurs when the scanner does not report a vulnerability that actually does exist.

A true positive alert occurs when the scanner correctly identifies a vulnerability that exists.

A true negative alert occurs when the scanner correctly identifies that no vulnerability exists.

Correct Answer: A. False positive

Practice Question 2 Explanation

This device is placed on the network and monitors network traffic, so you know that it is a network-based device. You also know that it is capable of blocking malicious traffic, so it is an intrusion prevention system. Therefore, this is a network-based intrusion prevention system (NIPS).

A network-based intrusion detection system (NIDS) also monitors the network, but it only alerts administrators to malicious activity and does not block it.

Host-based intrusion detection systems (HIDS) and host-based intrusion prevention systems (HIPS) are software installed on a single system, rather than devices that monitor an entire network.

Correct Answer: C. NIPS

CHAPTER 16

Network Security Infrastructure

Objective 4.3 Understand Network Security Infrastructure

Networks form the technological backbone of the modern organization, and security professionals must understand network security technologies. This expertise enables professionals to design and implement advanced strategies, ensuring not only the integrity and confidentiality of data but also the availability of network services, contributing significantly to the overall resilience of the organization.

In this chapter, you'll learn about the first two subobjectives of CC objective 4.3. The remaining material for this objective is covered in Chapter 17, "Cloud Computing." The following subobjectives are covered in this chapter:

▶ On-premises (e.g., power, data center/closets, Heating, Ventilation, and Air Conditioning (HVAC), environmental, fire suppression, redundancy, memorandum of understanding (MOU)/memorandum of agreement (MOA))

▶ Design (e.g., network segmentation (demilitarized zone (DMZ), virtual local area network (VLAN), virtual private network (VPN), micro-segmentation), defense in depth, Network Access Control (NAC) (segmentation for embedded systems, Internet of Things (IoT))

DATA CENTER PROTECTION

Data centers contain a wide variety of electronic equipment that is very sensitive to its operating environment. One of the major risks to this equipment comes in the form of environmental threats if the data center is not an appropriately controlled facility. Data center environmental controls seek to maintain a stable environment friendly to electronic equipment.

Air Temperature

The first environmental characteristic that data center engineers worry about is the air temperature. Electronic equipment generates a significant amount of heat, and if a data center does not have appropriate cooling equipment, the facility can become extremely hot. Excessive heat can dramatically reduce the life expectancy of servers and other electronic equipment, so data center facility managers invest heavily in maintaining a temperature friendly to that equipment. This investment requires massive cooling systems, such as the one shown in Figure 16.1 on a data center roof.

FIGURE 16.1 **HVAC systems on a data center roof**

Source: Alex/Adobe Stock Photos

The standards for data center cooling come from the American Society of Heating, Refrigerating and Air-Conditioning Engineers (ASHRAE). The experts now recommend what's called the *expanded environmental envelope*. It permits maintaining data centers at a temperature between 64.4 and 80.6 degrees Fahrenheit.

Humidity

Temperature isn't the only concern in managing the data center environment. Facilities staff must also carefully manage the humidity in the data center. If the humidity in the room is too high, condensation forms, and water is definitely not the friend of electronic equipment! If the humidity falls too low, static electricity builds up, which can be just as damaging.

Environmental specialists measure data center humidity using the dew point and recommend maintaining the facility at a dew point somewhere between 41.9 and 50.0 degrees Fahrenheit. That's the sweet spot that keeps both condensation and static electricity away.

Of course, you need to do more than monitor the temperature and humidity environment in your data centers. *Heating, ventilation, and air conditioning (HVAC) systems* allow you to control temperature and humidity, keeping them within acceptable ranges.

Fire

Fire is dangerous in any environment and can be particularly damaging in a facility filled with electrical equipment. For this reason, data center managers must design fire suppression systems that will extinguish a fire before it grows out of control.

Consider how fires start. In order for a fire to burn, three key ingredients are required: heat, oxygen, and fuel. These are known as the *fire triangle* and are shown in Figure 16.2. If you can deprive a fire of any one of these three elements, it will go out. The most common approach to fighting fires is the use of water, which deprives the fire of heat, but water is not effective against all types of fires and can damage electronic equipment.

FIGURE 16.2 **The fire triangle**

Data centers are normally protected by a facility-wide fire suppression system. This may be as simple as the water-based sprinkler system used throughout the rest of the facility, but this approach is risky. Water is very damaging to electronic equipment, and data center managers are justifiably nervous about having water in their facilities. An accidental discharge or burst pipe can lead to disaster.

The basic approach to water-based fire suppression is known as the *wet pipe* approach where the pipes are filled with water constantly. This is a high-risk approach in a data center because a pipe rupture could flood the facility.

Dry pipe systems try to remove water from the equation until an actual emergency strikes, lowering the risk to the facility. These systems use a valve that prevents water from entering pipes until a fire alarm triggers the suppression system. This approach minimizes the risk of burst pipes by keeping water out until the system detects a fire or is manually activated.

Some data centers use alternative fire suppression systems that fight fires with chemicals rather than water. While water deprives a fire of heat, chemical suppressants deprive the fire of oxygen. Of course, it's dangerous to deprive a room of oxygen if there are people present, so chemical suppressants must be used with care.

> **NOTE**
>
> If you run your own data center, you'll be responsible for providing environmental protection. If another team in your organization manages a data center that you use, you might create a memorandum of understanding (MOU) or memorandum of agreement (MOA) that outlines environmental requirements. If you purchase data center services from another organization, you should specify acceptable environmental conditions in a service level agreement, or SLA, with your service provider.

> **EXAM TIP**
>
> Power is also an important consideration when protecting data centers and is covered by exam objective 4.3. Chapter 8, "Business Continuity," discusses power redundancy controls.

NETWORK SECURITY ZONES

Well-designed networks use *firewalls* to group systems into network segments called *security zones* based on each system's security level. Firewalls are security devices that sit on a network and restrict the communications that can pass through them. Typical border firewalls have three network interfaces, as shown in Figure 16.3. They use these interfaces to connect three different security zones:

> ▶ One interface connects to the *Internet* or another untrusted network. This is the interface between the protected networks and the outside world. Generally speaking, firewalls allow many different kinds of connections out to this network when initiated by a system on more trusted networks, but they block most inbound connection attempts, allowing only those that meet the organization's security policy.

▶ A second interface connects to the organization's *intranet*. This is the internal network where most systems reside. This intranet zone may be further subdivided into segments for endpoint systems, wireless networks, guest networks, data center networks, and networks that meet other business needs. The firewall can be configured to control access between those subnets, or the organization can use additional firewalls to segment those networks.

▶ The third interface connects to the *demilitarized zone (DMZ)*. The DMZ is a network where you can place systems that must accept connections from the outside world, such as a mail or web server. Those systems are placed in a separate security zone because they have a higher risk of compromise. If an attacker compromises a DMZ screened subnet system, the firewall still blocks them from breaching the intranet.

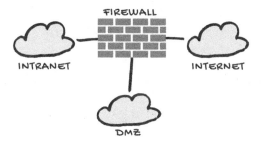

FIGURE 16.3 A network border firewall with three interfaces

SWITCHES, WAPs, AND ROUTERS

Networks carry all types of data over distances short and far. Whether it's a transatlantic videoconference or an email across the room, many different networks carry the 1s and 0s that make communications work. Switches and routers are the core building blocks of these networks.

Switches

Network engineers use *switches* to connect devices to networks. They are simple-looking devices, such as the switch shown in Figure 16.4, that contain a large number of network ports. Switches can be very small, with eight or fewer ports, or they can be quite large, with 500 or more ports. The switch shown in Figure 16.4 is a typical 48-port switch.

Switches are normally hidden away inside wiring closets and other secure locations. Each switch port is connected to one end of a network cable. Those cables then disappear into special pipes known as *conduits* for distribution around a building.

FIGURE 16.4 **A 48-port network switch**

Source: amorphis/Adobe Stock Photos

When the cable reaches the final destination, it usually terminates in a neat-looking wall keystone faceplate like the one shown in Figure 16.5. This provides an easy way for users and technicians to connect and disconnect computers from the network without damaging the cables inside the wall or having unsightly unused wires lying about the room.

FIGURE 16.5 **A network connection in a wall**

Source: Andrii/Adobe Stock Photos

WAPs

Some devices directly connect to switch ports through the use of wired networks. Many other devices don't use wires but instead depend on radio-based wireless networks. These networks are created by *wireless access points (WAPs)* like the one shown in Figure 16.6. These APs contain radios that send and receive network signals to and from mobile devices. The AP itself has a wired connection back to the switch, forming a bridge, allowing the wireless devices to connect to the rest of the network.

Routers

Routers play a higher-level role, connecting networks together by serving as a central aggregation point for network traffic heading to or from a large network. The router serves as the air traffic controller of the network, making decisions about the best paths for traffic to follow as it travels to its final destination. Routers also perform some security functions, using access control lists (ACLs) to limit the traffic that can enter or leave a network based on the organization's security policies.

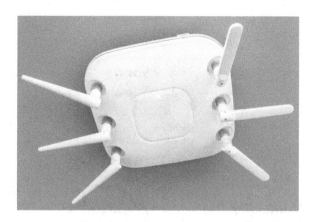

FIGURE 16.6 **A wireless access point (WAP)**

Source: v74/Adobe Stock Photos

NETWORK SEGMENTATION

Virtual LANs (VLANs) are an important network security control. VLANs enable you to logically group together related systems, regardless of where they normally exist on the network.

Diagrams of desired network layouts typically look something like the one shown in Figure 16.7, with different functional groups having different network locations. Users in the accounting department all share a network separate from users in the sales department and those in the IT department.

If your building and floor layout matched the network diagram in Figure 16.7 exactly, you'd be all set. More often than not, however, users from different departments are mingled together and departments are spread across buildings. That's where VLANs come into play. You can use them to connect users who are on different parts of the network to each other and to separate them from other users who might be geographically close. Figure 16.8 shows how this same network might be organized using VLANs.

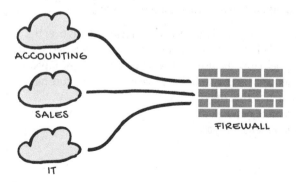

FIGURE 16.7 **A typical network diagram**

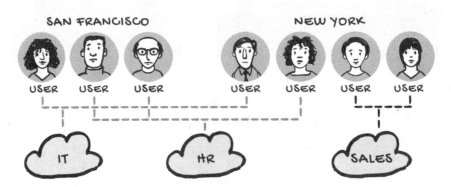

F I G U R E   1 6 . 8   **A typical VLAN layout**

VLANs are used to create *network segmentation*. This separates systems into networks consisting of similar systems, reducing the security risk by limiting the capability of unrelated systems to communicate with each other.

Microsegmentation is an extreme segmentation strategy that uses very small network segments that can be modified often to meet changing business requirements. These network segments can be created temporarily to allow two systems to communicate and then removed when they are no longer needed.

VIRTUAL PRIVATE NETWORKS

Virtual private networks (VPNs) provide two important network security functions to IT administrators:

> ▶ *Site-to-site VPNs* allow the secure interconnection of remote networks, such as connecting branch offices to corporate headquarters or each other.
> ▶ *Remote access VPNs* provide mobile workers with a mechanism to securely connect from remote locations back to the organization's network.

VPNs work by using encryption to create a virtual tunnel between two systems over the Internet. Everything that enters one end of the tunnel is encrypted, and then it is decrypted when it exits the other end of the tunnel. From the user's perspective, the network appears to function normally, but if an attacker gains access to traffic between the two secure networks, all they see is encrypted information that they can't read.

VPNs require an endpoint on the remote network that accepts VPN connections. Many different devices may serve as VPN endpoints, such as:

> ▶ Firewall
> ▶ Router

▶ Server

▶ Dedicated VPN concentrator

All of these approaches provide secure VPN connections, but organizations that have high volumes of VPN use often choose to use a dedicated VPN concentrator because these devices are very efficient at VPN connections and can manage high bandwidth traffic with ease. If you don't have a high volume of VPN traffic, you might choose to use the firewall, router, or server approach. If you go that way, be warned that VPN traffic requires resource-intensive encryption. Firewalls, routers, and servers, unlike VPN concentrators, usually don't contain specialized hardware that accelerates encryption. Using them as VPN endpoints can cause performance issues.

NETWORK ACCESS CONTROL

Network administrators normally need to restrict network access to authorized users and ensure that users only have access to resources appropriate to their roles. That's where *network access control (NAC)* plays an important role. NAC technology intercepts network traffic from devices that connect to a wired or wireless network and verifies that the system and user are authorized to connect to the network before allowing them to communicate with other systems.

NAC often uses an authentication protocol called *802.1x* to perform these access control tasks. The following three systems are involved in any 802.1x connection:

▶ The first is the device that wants to connect to the NAC-protected network. This device must be running a special piece of software called a *supplicant*. The supplicant is responsible for performing all of the NAC-related tasks on behalf of the user and system.

▶ The second device involved in the authentication is the switch that the device connects to, in the case of a wired network. This device, which receives credentials from the end user, is known as the authenticator in NAC terms. On a wireless network, the wireless controller serves as the authenticator.

▶ The third device is the backend authentication server. This is a centralized server that performs authentication for all of the authenticators on the network. In fact, it often performs authentication for many different services. NAC authentication is just one of those supported services.

Here's how they work together:

1. A user with a NAC supplicant attempts to join the network by plugging into a network jack, connecting to a VPN, or connecting to a wireless network.
2. The NAC supplicant provides the authenticator with the required authentication credentials.
3. When the authenticator receives those credentials, it passes them along to the authentication server for verification. This happens over a RADIUS connection.

4. If the credentials are authentic, the authentication server sends the authenticator a RADIUS Access-Accept message and the authenticator allows the device to access the network.
5. If the credentials don't verify correctly, the authentication server sends a RADIUS Access-Reject message and the user is often prompted to try again.

NAC can do more than just simple authentication, however. It can also perform two other tasks: role-based access control and posture checking.

Role-Based Access Control

In *role-based access control*, once the authenticator verifies the identity of the user through the authentication server, it also makes a decision about where to place the user on the network based on that user's identity.

For example, in a university environment, the authenticator might place students on a separate network from faculty and staff. This is normally done through the use of VLAN assignments. Students go on the student VLAN, and faculty and staff go on an administrative VLAN. Making these assignments separates different types of network users from each other.

Posture Checking

Network access control can also perform *posture checking*, also known as *endpoint compliance checking*. Networks using this technology verify that devices connecting to the network comply with the organization's security policy before granting broader access. Some of the checks performed during posture checking might include the following:

► Verifying that antivirus software is running on the system
► Validating that the antivirus software has current signatures
► Ensuring that the device has a properly configured host firewall
► Verifying that the device contains all recent security patches

If a device fails the posture check, it might be placed in a special *quarantine VLAN* where it has limited Internet access but no access to internal resources. The device can then use this limited access to obtain necessary patches and updates. Once the user remediates the device, the posture check repeats and NAC moves the device from the quarantine network to the appropriate user VLAN.

NAC posture checking can work using specialized software agents that are installed on the device or using an agentless approach that scans the device externally, seeking signs of insecure configuration or compromise.

NAC technology can work using an *in-band* approach, where the NAC device is directly involved in both making and enforcing the access control decision, or it can work using an *out-of-band* management approach, where the NAC device makes the enforcement decisions but it is left to the network switch, wireless access point, or other network components to enforce the decision.

INTERNET OF THINGS

Industrial systems aren't the only ones that have gone through a major change over the past decade. Embedded computer systems are now part of our everyday life as we adapt to the *Internet of Things (IoT)*. It's hard to walk around your house or the local consumer electronics store without seeing a huge number of devices that are now called "smart this" or "smart that." I now have in my home a smart television, a smart garage door, and even a smart sprinkler system. All that "smart" means in this context is that the devices are computer-controlled and connected to a network.

Embedded device technology began by taking some of the more common computing devices in our homes, such as game consoles and printers, and making them first network-connected and then wireless. Manufacturers quickly realized that we wanted connectivity to enable multiplayer games and printing without cables and then brought this technology into the home. From there, the possibilities were endless, and wireless smart devices spread throughout the home, even extending into the garage with the advent of smart cars that offer in-vehicle computing systems to the drivers and passengers.

IoT Security

All of these IoT devices come with security challenges as well.

First, it is often difficult for the consumer to update the software on these devices. While the devices might run slimmed down versions of traditional operating systems, they don't always have displays or keyboards, so users don't see that their so-called "smart" device is actually running an outdated copy of Windows 95!

Second, these devices connect to the same wireless networks that are used for personal productivity. If a smart device is compromised, it can be a gateway to the rest of the network.

Finally, smart devices often connect back to cloud services for command and control, creating a potential pathway onto the network for external attackers that bypasses the firewall.

IoT Network Segmentation

One way that you can ensure control diversity and redundancy for embedded systems is to place them within a secure network environment that is designed to protect smart devices from attack and protect other systems on the network from compromised smart devices. The tried-and-true way to protect suspect systems is the use of network segmentation. Network segmentation simply places untrusted devices on a network of their own, where they have no access to trusted systems.

In the context of embedded devices, that might look something like Figure 16.9. The standard corporate wired and wireless networks have laptops, desktops, and servers connected to them, and then a separate network, hanging off the firewall, contains embedded devices used to control an industrial process.

Does this look similar to anything you've already seen in your study of information security? If it looks like a firewall DMZ, there's a good reason for that—it's the same concept!

Placing embedded systems in an isolated DMZ allows them to access each other and the Internet but also allows you to strictly control that access as well as limit the access those devices have to other systems on your network.

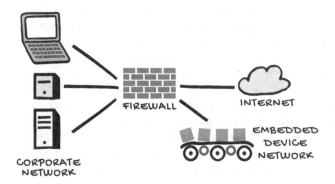

FIGURE 16.9 **IoT network segmentation**

Network segmentation is perhaps the most important control you can put in place to protect embedded systems.

EXAM ESSENTIALS

▶ Data centers should be carefully managed to protect the equipment that they contain. This includes maintaining temperature and humidity levels using heating, ventilation, and air conditioning (HVAC) systems and maintaining fire suppression controls.

▶ Routers and switches are the devices that form the backbone of the modern network. Networked devices connect to a switch via a network cable or to a wireless access point via a Wi-Fi connection. Switches connect to each other and to routers. Routers send traffic between switches on the internal network and the Internet.

▶ Firewalls are security devices that restrict the traffic that can enter and leave a network. Border firewalls connect three zones. The Internet zone connects the organization to the Internet. The intranet zone hosts internal systems. The DMZ hosts systems that can be accessed by the general public.

▶ Network access control (NAC) technology intercepts network traffic from devices that connect to a wired or wireless network and verifies that the system and user are authorized to connect to the network before allowing them to communicate with other systems.

Practice Question 1

You are concerned about the ability of outside individuals to access your internal network and would like to use a network device to restrict this access. Which one of the following devices would best meet this need?

A. Firewall
B. Router
C. Switch
D. Access point

Practice Question 2

You are placing a new server on your organization's network. The server will host a public website and needs to be accessed by both internal employees and the public. What is the most appropriate network zone for this server?

A. Internet
B. DMZ
C. Intranet
D. Extranet

Practice Question 1 Explanation

Looking at this question, you should be able to immediately eliminate two of the answer choices. Switches are components of an internal network; they are not connected to external networks and would not be used to control access into a network. Wireless access points are also internal network components used to connect wireless devices to the wired network. You can eliminate both of these options as possible answer choices.

That leaves two devices that do connect to external networks: firewalls and routers. The reality is that both firewalls and routers have the potential to fulfill this requirement. They both have filtering capabilities that can block unwanted external traffic. To answer this question correctly, focus on the word *best* that appears in the final sentence. The question is not asking which device *can* meet this need; it's asking which device can *best* meet this need. While routers do have limited filtering capability, they are not designed for this purpose. Firewalls, on the other hand, are designed specifically to restrict network traffic, making a firewall the best solution to this problem.

Correct Answer: A. Firewall

Practice Question 2 Explanation

The key to answering this question correctly is realizing that the server requires public access. Any server in your organization that will be accessed by the general public should be placed in the DMZ.

Servers should never be placed in the Internet zone, as this zone is completely unprotected by the firewall.

Servers should be placed on the intranet if they will be accessed only by internal users. Since this server must also be accessed by the general public, it is not appropriate to place it on the intranet.

Servers should be placed on an extranet if they will be accessed only by internal users and vendor partners. Since this server must also be accessed by the general public, it is not appropriate to place it on the extranet.

Correct Answer: B. DMZ

CHAPTER 17

Cloud Computing
Objective 4.3 Understand Network Security Infrastructure

Cloud computing is the most transformative development in information technology in the past decade. Organizations around the world are retooling their entire IT strategies to embrace the cloud, and this change is causing disruptive impact across all sectors of technology.

In this chapter, you'll learn about the third subobjective of CC objective 4.3. The remaining material for this objective is covered in Chapter 16, "Network Security Infrastructure." The following subobjective is covered in this chapter:

▶ **Cloud (e.g., service-level agreement (SLA), managed service provider (MSP), Software as a Service (SaaS), Infrastructure as a Service (IaaS), Platform as a Service (PaaS), hybrid)**

CLOUD COMPUTING

Cloud computing is the delivery of computing services to users over a network. Or, more formally, the National Institute of Standards and Technology (NIST) defines cloud computing as follows:

> A model for enabling ubiquitous, convenient, on-demand network access to a shared pool of configurable computing resources (e.g., networks, servers, storage, applications, and services) that can be rapidly provisioned and released with minimal management effort or service provider interaction.

Drivers for Cloud Computing

Organizations choose the cloud for some or all of their IT workloads for a variety of different reasons.

First, the cloud offers *on-demand* self-service computing. This means that technologists can access cloud resources almost immediately when they need them to do their job. That's an incredible increase in agility for individual contributors and, by extension, the organization. Before the era of on-demand computing, a technologist who wanted to try out a new idea might have to spec out the servers required to implement the idea, gain funding approval, order the hardware, wait for it to arrive, physically install it, and configure an operating system before getting down to work. That might have taken weeks, whereas today the same tasks can be accomplished in the cloud in a matter of seconds. On-demand self-service computing is a true game changer.

Cloud solutions also provide *scalability*. This means that, as the demand on a service increases, customers can easily increase the capacity available to them. This can occur in two different ways:

▶ *Horizontal scaling* refers to adding more servers to your pool. If you run a website that supports 2,000 concurrent users with two servers, you might add a new server every time your typical usage increases by another 1,000 users. Cloud computing makes this quite easy, as you can just replicate your existing server with a few clicks.

▶ *Vertical scaling* refers to increasing the capacity of your existing servers. For example, you might change the number of CPU cores or the amount of memory assigned to a server. In the physical world, this means opening up a server and adding physical hardware. In the cloud, you can just click a few buttons and add memory or compute capacity.

The cloud also offers rapid *elasticity*. Elasticity is a concept that is closely related to scalability. It refers to both increasing and decreasing capacity as short-term needs fluctuate. If your website starts to experience a burst in activity, elasticity enables you to automatically add servers until that capacity is met and then remove those servers when the capacity is no longer needed.

The cloud offers broad network access. If you have the ability to access the Internet, you can connect to public cloud solutions from wherever you are—in the office, at a coffee shop, or on the road.

Finally, the cloud offers *measured service* as one of its defining characteristics. This means that almost everything you do in the cloud is metered. Cloud providers measure the number of seconds you use a virtual server, the amount of disk space you consume, the number of function calls you make, and many other measures. This allows them to charge you for precisely the services you use—no more and no less. The measured service model is a little intimidating when you first encounter it, but it provides cloud customers with the ability to manage their utilization effectively and achieve the economic benefits of the cloud.

CLOUD DEPLOYMENT MODELS

When deploying cloud services, organizations have four primary choices: private cloud computing, public cloud computing, hybrid cloud computing, and community cloud computing.

Private Cloud

In the *private cloud* approach, the organization builds and runs its own cloud infrastructure or pays another organization to do so on its behalf. Organizations using the private cloud model want to gain the flexibility, scalability, agility, and cost-effectiveness of the cloud but do not want to share computing resources with other organizations.

Public Cloud

The *public cloud* uses a different approach: the *multitenancy* model. In this approach, cloud providers build massive infrastructures in their data centers and then make those resources available to all comers. The same physical hardware may be running workloads for many different customers at the same time.

Multitenancy simply means that many different customers share use of the same computing resources. The physical servers that support your workloads might be the same as the physical servers supporting your neighbor's workloads.

In an ideal world, an individual customer should never see the impact of multitenancy. Servers should appear completely independent of each other and enforce the principle of *isolation*. From a security perspective, one customer should never be able to see data belonging to another customer. From a performance perspective, the actions that one customer takes should never impact the actions of another customer. Preserving isolation is the core crucial security task of a cloud service provider.

Of course, sometimes this concept breaks down. If customers do suddenly have simultaneous demands for resources that exceed the total capacity of the environment, performance degrades. This causes slowdowns and outages. Preventing this situation is one of the key operational tasks of a cloud service provider, and they work hard to manage workload allocation to prevent this from happening.

When organizations use public cloud resources, they must understand that security in the public cloud follows a shared responsibility model. Depending on the nature of the cloud service, the cloud provider is responsible for some areas of security, while the customer is responsible for other areas. For example, if you purchase a cloud storage service, it's your responsibility to know what data you're sending to the service and probably to configure access control policies that say who can access your data. It's the provider's responsibility to encrypt data under their care and correctly implement your access control policies.

CLOUD CONNECTIVITY

No matter which cloud deployment model you use, you'll need some way to connect your employees, office buildings, and/or physical data centers to your cloud environment. You can choose to do this over a normal Internet connection, but many companies choose to add a layer of security to protect that traffic from prying eyes.

The most cost-effective way to do this is to create a virtual private network (VPN) connection between your existing systems and networks to the cloud data center. If you'd like higher bandwidth, you can choose to purchase a private direct connection from your cloud provider to your enterprise network.

Hybrid Cloud

Organizations adopting a *hybrid cloud* approach use a combination of public and private cloud computing. In this model, they can use the public cloud for some computing workloads, but they also operate their own private cloud for some workloads, often because of data sensitivity concerns.

Community Cloud

One additional cloud model is possible, but it is not frequently used. *Community clouds* are similar to private clouds in that they are not open to the general public, but they are shared among several or many organizations that are related to each other in a common community. For example, a group of colleges and universities might get together and create a community cloud that provides shared computing resources for faculty and students at all participating schools.

EXAM TIP

When taking the CC exam, remember that no one cloud model is inherently superior to the others. Some organizations might want to use a public cloud-heavy approach to achieve greater cost savings, while others might have regulatory requirements that prohibit the use of shared tenancy computing.

CLOUD SERVICE CATEGORIES

Cloud services come in a variety of different categories. This section discusses the four major service categories of cloud computing that you'll need to know for the CC exam: software as a service (SaaS), infrastructure as a service (IaaS), platform as a service (PaaS), and desktop as a service (DaaS).

Software as a Service (SaaS)

In a *software as a service (SaaS)* model, the public cloud provider delivers an entire application to its customers. Customers don't need to worry about processing, storage, networking, or any of the infrastructure details of the cloud service. The vendor writes the application, configures the servers, and basically gets everything running for customers, who then simply use the service. Very often these services are accessed through a standard web browser, so very little, if any, configuration is required on the customer's end.

Common examples of SaaS applications include email delivered by Google Workspace or Microsoft 365, and storage services that facilitate collaboration and synchronization across devices, such as Box and Dropbox. SaaS applications can also be very specialized, such as credit card processing services and travel and expense reporting management.

Infrastructure as a Service (IaaS)

Customers of *infrastructure as a service (IaaS)* vendors purchase basic computing resources from vendors and piece them together to create customized IT solutions. For example, IaaS vendors might provide compute capacity, data storage, and other basic infrastructure building blocks. The three major vendors in the IaaS space are Amazon Web Services, Microsoft Azure, and Google Cloud Platform.

Platform as a Service (PaaS)

In the third tier of public cloud computing, *platform as a service (PaaS)*, vendors provide customers with a platform where they can run their own application code without worrying about server configuration. This is a middle ground between IaaS and SaaS. Users don't need to worry about managing servers, but they are still running their own code.

Desktop as a Service (DaaS)

As companies turn to telecommuting and other remote work arrangements, the demand increases for technologies that allow those users to easily interact with enterprise systems from their homes and other locations.

Desktop as a service (DaaS) solutions take the power of virtualization and apply it to desktop technology. Users can use any system of their choice to access a desktop environment that is running on a remote server. This might be a DaaS solution running in the company's own data center or a cloud-based DaaS product, such as Amazon's WorkSpaces.

EXAM TIP

As you prepare for the CC exam, be ready to review a scenario that describes a cloud service and then select the appropriate cloud service category or deployment model described in that scenario.

SECURITY AND THE SHARED RESPONSIBILITY MODEL

Security professionals need to think about security much differently in a cloud computing model. The shared responsibility model requires that both vendors and customers take responsibility for different elements of security.

> ▶ In an IaaS approach, the vendor is responsible for managing the security of their hardware and data center. Customers configure the operating system, applications, and data, so securing those elements is primarily a customer responsibility.
>
> ▶ In a PaaS approach, the customer is still responsible for the data and applications but doesn't directly interact with the operating system, so that responsibility shifts to the vendor.
>
> ▶ In a SaaS approach, the vendor manages almost everything, and the only responsibility that the customer has is knowing what data is stored in the service and applying appropriate access controls.

Understanding this shared responsibility model is a critical responsibility for security professionals working in a public cloud environment.

AUTOMATION AND ORCHESTRATION

Cloud *orchestration* creates automated workflows for managing cloud environments. It allows cloud administrators to quickly and easily create workloads, shift operations between environments, and perform a variety of other administrative tasks.

Cloud orchestration builds on the concept of *infrastructure as code (IaC)*. This is the idea that administrators should never build or manage resources using the command line or graphical interfaces. Instead, they should write code that performs those actions for them. The key benefit here is that the code is then reusable. If you build a web server by hand, then when you need to rebuild that web server, you need to follow that same laborious process all over again. On the other hand, if you write a script to build your web server, the next time you need a similar server, you can just rerun that script. Or, better yet, you can have your cloud orchestration solution automatically execute that script when necessary.

Cloud orchestration relies on the robust *application programming interfaces (APIs)* offered by cloud providers. These APIs allow any action that you can perform through the web interface to also be performed as a programmatic function call. APIs are available for all major cloud providers and support a variety of programming languages.

Organizations implementing cloud orchestration can choose to use the native capabilities offered by their primary cloud service provider, or they can choose to implement a third-party cloud orchestration solution. The primary benefit of this approach is that third-party products often support many different cloud providers and can work across different cloud solutions.

VENDOR RELATIONSHIPS

Vendors play an important role in the information technology operations of every organization. Whether it's the simple purchasing of hardware or software from an external company or the provision of cloud computing services from a strategic partner, vendors are integral in providing the IT services that you offer your customers. Security professionals must pay careful attention to managing these business partnerships in a way that protects the confidentiality, integrity, and availability of their organization's information and IT systems. This process is known as conducting vendor due diligence.

Perhaps the most important rule of thumb is that you should always ensure that vendors follow security policies and procedures that are at least as effective as you would apply in your own environment. Vendors extend your organization's technology environment, and if they handle data on your behalf, you should expect that they execute the same degree of care that you would in your own operations. Otherwise, vendors can become the weak link in the supply chain and jeopardize your security objectives.

Managed Service Providers

As organizations seek to outsource components of their technology infrastructure, they often turn to *managed service providers (MSPs)* to perform tasks that they either consider commodities or believe can be more efficiently and effectively performed by a third party. In some cases, this means turning to outside firms to provide critical security services.

Vendors that provide security services for other organizations are known as *managed security service providers (MSSPs)*. MSSPs play a critical role in an organization's security program and should be carefully monitored to ensure that they are living up to their status as trusted partners and are effectively meeting the organization's security objectives.

MSSPs vary widely in the scope of their services and can perform different services for different clients. Some MSSPs take over complete responsibility for managing an organization's security infrastructure. Others perform a specific task, such as log monitoring, firewall and network management, or identity and access management.

Vendor Agreements

One of the most important components of managing vendor relationships is ensuring that appropriate agreements are in place to ensure interoperability and require that the vendor provide a level of service consistent with the customer's expectations.

Non-Disclosure Agreements
Non-disclosure agreements (NDAs) are typically the first document signed as two organizations explore a business partnership. These documents assure the firms that they will keep each other's information confidential.

Service Level Agreements

As an organization begins to evaluate a new vendor relationship, it should establish *service level requirements (SLRs)* that describe the organization's expectations of the vendor during the relationship. These requirements should address any concerns that the customer has about the quality of service provided by the vendor.

For example, service level requirements can include system response time, availability of service, data preservation requirements, or any other parameter specified by the customer.

Once an organization negotiates these requirements with the vendor, it should document the results in a *service level agreement (SLA)*. The SLA is a written contract between the vendor and the customer that describes the conditions of service and the penalties the vendor will incur for failure to maintain the agreed-upon service level.

Memorandum of Understanding

A *memorandum of understanding (MOU)* is simply a letter written to document aspects of the relationship. MOUs are commonly used when a legal dispute is unlikely but the customer and vendor still want to document their relationship to avoid future misunderstandings. MOUs are commonly used in cases where an internal service provider is offering a service to a customer that is in a different business unit of the same company.

EXAM ESSENTIALS

▶ Cloud customers can choose from four deployment models. Public cloud offerings use shared hardware for many customers in a multitenant approach. Private cloud offerings dedicate hardware to a single customer. Community cloud offerings are open only to members of a specific community. Hybrid cloud offerings mix resources from two or more deployment models.

▶ Cloud services come in four categories: software as a service (SaaS), platform as a service (PaaS), infrastructure as a service (IaaS), and desktop as a service (DaaS).

▶ Automation and orchestration improve the efficiency of managing cloud resources. A common approach to this is the use of an infrastructure as code (IaC) model to script the creation and configuration of cloud resources.

Practice Question 1

Your organization is shifting a series of workloads from an on-premises data center to the cloud. You are working with a vendor that allows you to start up virtual server instances as needed, and then you configure those servers to meet your business requirements. Which cloud service category does this describe?

A. PaaS
B. SaaS
C. DaaS
D. IaaS

Practice Question 2

Your organization recently signed a contract with a major IaaS provider for services that will be provided in a multitenancy model. As part of the setup process, you are working with the provider to run a dedicated fiber connection directly from your organization's headquarters campus to the cloud provider's data center. Which cloud deployment model are you using?

A. Private cloud
B. Community cloud
C. Hybrid cloud
D. Public cloud

Practice Question 1 Explanation

This is an example of an infrastructure as a service (IaaS) cloud offering because the service provider is offering you virtual server instances (a core infrastructure component), and then you are configuring those server instances to meet the needs of your organization.

In a software as a service (SaaS) approach, the provider would sell you a complete application that runs in the cloud, and you would not configure any of the underlying infrastructure yourself.

In a platform as a service (PaaS) approach, the provider would allow you to run your own application code on a platform that they manage. You still would not manage any of the underlying infrastructure.

Finally, in a desktop as a service (DaaS) offering, the cloud provider offers end-user productivity desktops that users can use in place of personal computers. That is not the situation described in this scenario.

Correct Answer: D. IaaS

Practice Question 2 Explanation

The key to answering this question correctly is to note that the services are provided in a multitenancy environment. This means that many different customers are sharing the same hardware and that this is a public cloud service offering.

A private cloud approach would use resources dedicated only to your organization and would not be multitenant. You do have a dedicated, private fiber connection to the cloud provider, but the cloud service being provided is still a public cloud offering.

There is no indication in the scenario that you are using these services in conjunction with a private cloud, which would make it a hybrid approach, or that you are using an offering open only to customers with a common background, which would make it a community cloud model.

Correct Answer: D. Public cloud

Domain 5: Security Operations

Security Operations is the fifth domain of ISC2's Certified in Cybersecurity exam. It provides the knowledge that entry-level cybersecurity professionals need to know about everyday cybersecurity operations. This domain includes the following four objectives:

5.1 Understand data security

5.2 Understand system hardening

5.3 Understand best practice security policies

5.4 Understand security awareness training

Questions from this domain make up 18 percent of the questions on the CC exam, so you should expect to see 18 questions on your test covering the material in this part.

CHAPTER 18

Encryption
Objective 5.1 Understand Data Security

Encryption protects information from prying eyes by making it unreadable to anyone who does not have the required decryption key. We use encryption to protect data that is at rest on a storage device or in transit over a network.

In this chapter, you'll learn about the first subobjective of CC objective 5.1. The remaining material for this objective is covered in Chapter 19, "Data Handling," and Chapter 20, "Logging and Monitoring." The following subobjective is covered in this chapter:

▶ **Encryption (e.g., symmetric, asymmetric, hashing)**

CRYPTOGRAPHY

Encryption is one of the most important security controls that you can use to protect the confidentiality of your data. Encryption uses mathematical operations to transform information into a format where it is unreadable by anyone other than the authorized user.

> **EXAM TIP**
>
> The math behind encryption is pretty complex, but the good news is that you won't be responsible for any of that math on the CC exam. You just need to know the basics of what encryption does and how you can use it to protect your organization.

Encrypting Data

When encrypting data, you start with some *plaintext* information. Plain text is just a fancy way of saying that the information is in its normal form; anyone who looks at the data can read it. Figure 18.1 shows an example of a file containing plain text—the first paragraph from this chapter.

You then take that information and use an encryption algorithm in combination with an encryption key to encrypt the data. The algorithm is the mathematical formula for the encryption, and the key is basically the password to the data. Once the plaintext data has been encrypted, it is referred to as *ciphertext*. Figure 18.2 shows the ciphertext obtained by encrypting the plaintext message shown in Figure 18.1.

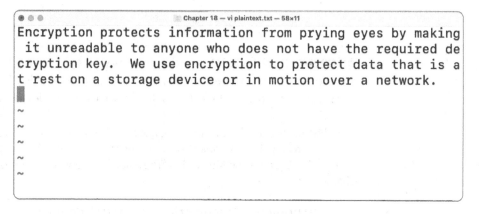

FIGURE 18.1 A plaintext message

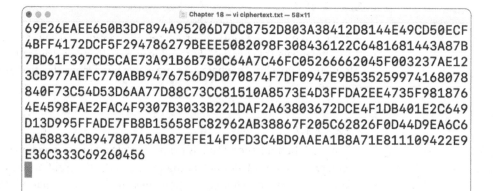

FIGURE 18.2 The ciphertext message obtained by encrypting the plain text in Figure 18.1

That ciphertext data is completely unreadable to anyone who examines it. It just looks like nonsense. This stays true until the data has been decrypted.

Decrypting Data

When someone wants to *decrypt* the ciphertext and turn it back into plain text, they use the decryption algorithm and the decryption key to perform that transformation. If they don't know the correct decryption key, the decryption simply won't work. So, protecting the key is vital. As long as unauthorized users don't have access to the decryption key, they won't have access to the data.

ENCRYPTION ALGORITHMS

There are many different kinds of encryption algorithms, and there are different ways to categorize them. Two of the major categories of encryption algorithms are *symmetric algorithms* and *asymmetric algorithms*.

You're probably already familiar with the concept of symmetry, meaning that two things are the same. Symmetric shapes have two sides that, when divided along an axis, are identical. Figure 18.3 shows examples of some symmetric shapes.

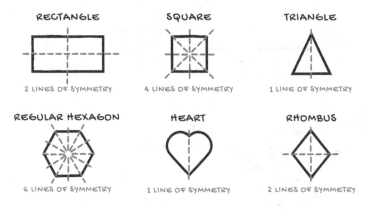

FIGURE 18.3 **Examples of symmetric shapes**

In cryptography, symmetry relates to keys rather than shapes.

Symmetric Encryption

In symmetric encryption algorithms, also known as shared secret encryption algorithms, the encryption and decryption operations use the same key. If one user encrypts a message using the secret key "Apple," a second user would have to decrypt the message with that same key. It's a shared secret. You can think of a shared secret key as the password to a message.

Let's say Alice and Bob want to communicate with each other. If they both know the shared secret, they can exchange encrypted messages with each other. This works great when only two people are involved. They can simply agree on an encryption key and use it with each other, as shown in Figure 18.4.

FIGURE 18.4 Symmetric encryption with two individuals

If three people are involved, things change a little bit. Alice and Bob can still use their shared secret to communicate with each other privately, but now Charlie joins the picture and wants to be able to communicate with Alice or Bob, as shown in Figure 18.5. Each person in the group wants the ability to communicate privately with any other member of the group.

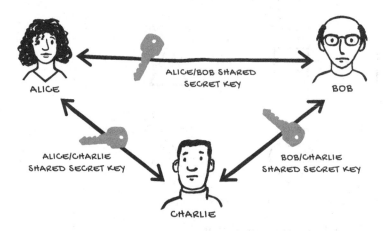

FIGURE 18.5 Symmetric encryption with three individuals

Alice has a way to communicate with Bob, but a second key is needed that allows her to communicate privately with Charlie. However, there is still a missing link. Bob and Charlie need a third key to communicate with each other. So, in order for these three people to communicate, three keys are required.

As groups get larger, more and more keys are required to facilitate the communication. There's a formula that computes the number of keys required for symmetric cryptography.

Where n is the number of people who want to communicate, the number of keys required, k, is equal to:

$$n(n-1) \div 2$$

As you can see in Figure 18.6, when larger groups are involved, symmetric cryptography starts to require an unmanageable number of keys. For example, an organization with 10,000 employees would need almost 50 million encryption keys! If a new person were to join the organization, the organization would need to generate 10,000 new keys for that person to communicate with other employees—and then distribute those 10,000 keys to every other employee in the organization!

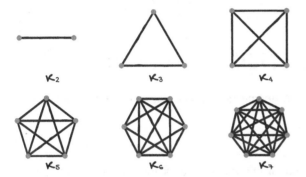

FIGURE 18.6 **Symmetric encryption with larger groups**

Asymmetric Encryption

Asymmetric cryptography solves the problem of scaling to large groups by using the concept of key pairs.

Each user gets two keys:

▶ A *public key* that they can freely distribute to anyone they want to communicate with
▶ A *private key* that they keep secret

In asymmetric cryptography, anything that is encrypted with one key from the pair can be decrypted with the other key from that pair. For normal communications, the sender of the message would encrypt it with the recipient's public key, which is publicly known. The recipient would then use their private key to decrypt the message.

> **EXAM NOTE**
>
> Remember that in asymmetric cryptography, the keys must be from the same pair! If Bob encrypts a message for Alice, he uses Alice's public key, and then Alice uses her own private key to decrypt the message because Alice's public and private key come from the same pair. People get this confused on the exam all the time.

Asymmetric cryptography is slower than symmetric cryptography, but it solves the problem of creating keys for large organizations. Only two keys are needed for each user. This results in much more manageable key counts for large organizations!

EXAM NOTE

As you prepare to answer exam questions, you should be familiar with the most common examples of symmetric and asymmetric encryption algorithms. The Advanced Encryption Standard (AES) is the most common symmetric encryption algorithm. The Rivest Shamir Adleman (RSA) algorithm is the most common asymmetric encryption algorithm.

USES OF ENCRYPTION

Encryption is used in two different environments: to protect data at rest and to protect data in transit.

Data at Rest

Data at rest is simply stored data. You can encrypt individual files, entire disks, or the contents of a mobile device. If someone gains access to one of those encrypted files, disks, or mobile devices, you don't need to worry about the encrypted data because they won't have access to the decryption key.

Full-disk encryption (FDE) is a technology built into some operating systems that automatically encrypts all of the data stored on a device. FDE technology is particularly useful for laptops, tablets, smartphones, and other devices that might be lost or stolen. Someone who steals the device will not be able to access the data it contains if that data is protected by full-disk encryption.

Data in Transit

Data in transit is data that's moving over a network. You can protect this data as well by using encryption.

When you access a website using the standard *HTTP* protocol, that data is unencrypted, and anyone who observes your network activity can eavesdrop on your web use. However, if you use the secure *HTTPS* protocol, that connection is encrypted, and the data being sent over the network is safe from prying eyes.

You can use the same encryption technology to protect the data being sent in email messages, from mobile applications to their servers, or even protect entire network connections with encryption using a *virtual private network (VPN)*.

HASH FUNCTIONS

Hash functions are extremely important to the use of public key cryptography and, in particular, to the creation of digital signatures and digital certificates. Let me start by giving you the technical definition of a hash function, and then I'll explain it piece by piece. A hash function is a one-way function that consistently transforms a variable-length input into a unique, fixed-length output.

Let's pick apart that definition:

> ▶ Hash functions are one-way functions. That means you can't reverse the process of hashing. If you have content, you can use a hash function to calculate the hash value of that content, but you can't go the other way around. If you have a hash value, you can't use it to figure out the original text.
> ▶ Hash functions map variable-length input to fixed-length outputs. That simply means that you can send input of any length to a hash function and the hashes that it produces will always be the same length. Feed in two words or an entire book, and you'll get output that is the same length. That length depends on the hash function, but it will always be fixed.
> ▶ Hash functions also produce unique output. That means that you should not be able to find two different inputs that produce the same hash value as output.
> ▶ Hash functions are repeatable in that you always get the same output from hashing the same input using the same hash function.

In order for a hash function to be effective, it must meet all four of those criteria. A hash function can fail in one of the following two ways:

> ▶ First, if the hash function is reversible, it is not secure. Hash values can become public, so you don't want any way for someone seeing the hash value to determine the content of a message.
> ▶ The more common way that a hash function will fail is that someone will demonstrate that it is not collision-resistant. That means that it doesn't achieve the "unique output" part of the definition and it is possible to find two inputs that produce the same hash output. If that were the case, it would make it possible to forge digital signatures and digital certificates. That's clearly undesirable!

EXAM NOTE

When taking the CC exam, you should be familiar with the details of common hash functions, with particular attention to knowing which hash functions are still considered secure.

MD5

Ron Rivest created the *Message Digest 5 (MD5)* hash function in 1991. That's the same Rivest who coinvented the RSA encryption algorithm. MD5 was the fifth in a series of hash functions that became more and more secure. MD5 replaced the MD4 algorithm after research showed that MD4 was insecure.

> **NOTE**
>
> *Message digest* is just another term for *hash*. The two terms mean the same thing and can be used interchangeably.

MD5 produces a 128-bit hash.

Over the years, cryptanalysts discovered a series of flaws in the MD5 algorithm that chipped away at its collision resistance. In 2013, three cryptanalysts discovered a technique that breaks MD5's collision resistance in less than a second on a store-bought computer. Therefore, MD5 is no longer considered secure and should not be used. However, many systems still rely on MD5 for secure applications—a very bad idea!

SHA

The *Secure Hash Algorithm (SHA)* is another series of hash functions approved by the National Institute of Standards and Technology (NIST) for use in federal computing applications.

The first version of SHA, SHA-1, produces a 160-bit hash value. Cryptanalysts have discovered increasingly severe flaws in SHA-1 over the past few years and no longer consider SHA-1 secure for use.

SHA-2 replaced SHA-1 and is actually a family of six different hash algorithms. The different algorithms of SHA-2 have different hash lengths, which include 224-, 256-, 384-, and 512-bit hashes.

All of the SHA-2 algorithms are mathematically similar to SHA-1 and MD5 and are theoretically susceptible to the same flaws that broke those algorithms. Some attacks now exist against certain configurations of SHA-2, but the algorithm is still widely used.

NIST recognized that the mathematical similarity between SHA-2 and other, insecure, algorithms represents a future risk to SHA-2 and, thinking ahead, they began a competition to select a third version of SHA, SHA-3, in 2007. In 2012, NIST announced the selection of the Keccak algorithm as the SHA-3 standard.

SHA-3 uses a completely different mathematical technique and can actually produce a hash of any desired length. The length is set by the person computing the hash, so Keccak still satisfies the fixed-length criteria. It just allows the use of *any* fixed-length output.

> **EXAM TIP**
>
> When taking the CC exam, you should understand that encryption is used to transform plain text into ciphertext and that it protects both data at rest—stored in files or on devices—and data in transit as it is being sent over a network.

EXAM ESSENTIALS

▶ Encryption is the process of transforming plaintext information into ciphertext that can't be read by unauthorized individuals. Decryption uses a decryption key to convert ciphertext back into plain text.

▶ Encryption can be used to protect data at rest by encrypting individual files or folders. Full-disk encryption (FDE) uses encryption to protect the entire contents of a device.

▶ Encryption can be used to protect data in transit by encrypting it as it travels over a network. The HTTPS protocol encrypts web traffic and is a secure alternative to the unencrypted HTTP protocol. Virtual private networks (VPNs) encrypt entire network connections.

▶ Symmetric encryption algorithms, such as AES, use the same key to encrypt and decrypt messages. Asymmetric encryption algorithms, such as RSA, use public and private key pairs.

▶ Hash functions are one-way functions that transform a variable-length input into a unique, fixed-length output.

Practice Question 1

You are concerned that users traveling with laptops will have those devices stolen while in transit. Which encryption technology would best protect the data stored on those laptops?

A. HTTPS

B. HTTP

C. VPN

D. FDE

Practice Question 2

You have a group of remote users who need to access the corporate network from their homes. You would like to protect the information that they send back and forth to the corporate network, regardless of the application that they use. Which encryption technology would best meet this need?

A. HTTPS

B. HTTP

C. VPN

D. FDE

Practice Question 1 Explanation

This question is asking you to identify an encryption technology that will protect data at rest and, in particular, the entire contents of a laptop. Full-disk encryption (FDE) is designed for this use case. FDE encrypts an entire hard drive, rendering the contents inaccessible to an unauthorized individual who steals or finds the device.

HTTP is not an encrypted protocol. HTTPS is a secure, encrypted alternative to HTTP, but it is used to protect web traffic, which is an example of data in transit, and would not be effective in protecting a lost or stolen laptop.

Similarly, virtual private networks (VPNs) protect network communications and would not be effective in protecting a lost or stolen laptop.

Correct Answer: D. FDE

Practice Question 2 Explanation

You can begin by eliminating full-disk encryption (FDE) as an answer choice because FDE is designed to protect the contents of a disk—data at rest. It does not protect data in transit over a network.

The HTTP protocol is unencrypted, so it does not provide any protection. HTTPS is a secure, encrypted alternative to HTTP, but it is used only to protect web traffic. It would protect any web communications from the remote users but would not protect other applications.

Virtual private networks (VPNs) create secure network connections between two locations and would be an effective means of protecting the communications of these remote users.

Correct Answer: C. VPN

CHAPTER 19

Data Handling
Objective 5.1 Understand Data Security

Data security is an integral aspect of maintaining an organization's integrity and trust. Understanding how to manage data throughout its life cycle—from creation to destruction—is a critical skill for any security professional. This includes not only knowing how to securely store, use, and share data but also how to correctly archive and ultimately destroy data when it's no longer needed.

In this chapter, you'll learn about the second subobjective of CC objective 5.1. The remaining material for this objective is covered in Chapter 18, "Encryption," and Chapter 20, "Logging and Monitoring." The following subobjective is covered in this chapter:

▶ **Data handling (e.g., destruction, retention, classification, labeling)**

DATA LIFE CYCLE

The data life cycle shown in Figure 19.1 is a useful way to understand the process that data goes through within an organization. It covers everything from the time data is first created until the time it is eventually destroyed. You can think of it as a way of viewing the data journey from cradle to grave.

FIGURE 19.1 Data life cycle

Create

In the first stage of the life cycle, *create*, the organization generates new data either in an on-premises system or in the cloud. The create stage also includes modifications to existing data.

Store

From there, the second stage of the life cycle is *store*. In this stage, the organization places the data into one or more storage systems. Again, these can be either on premises or at a cloud service provider.

Use

The next stage, *use*, is where the active use of data takes place. Users and systems view and process data in this stage.

Share

In the fourth stage, *share*, the data is made available to other people through one or more sharing mechanisms. This might include providing customers with a link to a file, modifying access controls so that other employees can view it, or other similar actions.

Archive

When the data is no longer being actively used, it moves to the fifth stage, *archive*. In this stage, data is retained in long-term storage where it is not immediately accessible but can be restored to active use if necessary.

The archiving of data should follow an organization's *data retention* policy. This policy should state how long the organization will preserve different types of records and when they should be destroyed. As a general practice, organizations should dispose of records when they are no longer necessary for a legitimate business purpose.

Destroy

In the final stage of the life cycle, *destroy*, data is eventually destroyed when it is no longer needed. This destruction should take place using a secure disposal method.

Data destruction must be done in a secure manner to avoid situations where an attacker obtains paper or electronic media and then manages to reconstruct sensitive data that still exists on that media in some form.

Destroying Electronic Records

The National Institute of Standards and Technology (NIST) provides a set of guidelines for secure media sanitization in its Special Publication 800-88. It includes three different activities for sanitizing electronic media:

> ▶ *Clearing*, the most basic sanitization technique, consists simply of writing new data to the device that overwrites sensitive data. Clearing is effective against most types of casual analysis.

▶ *Purging* is similar to clearing but uses more advanced techniques and takes longer. Purging might use cryptographic functions to obscure media on disk. Purging also includes the use of degaussing techniques, which apply strong magnetic fields to securely overwrite data.

▶ *Destroying* is the ultimate type of data sanitization. You shred, pulverize, melt, incinerate, or otherwise completely destroy the media so that it is totally impossible for someone to reconstruct it. The downside of destruction, of course, is that you can't reuse the media as you would with clearing or purging.

Figure 19.2 shows a flowchart that can help you make decisions about which sanitization technique to use. It comes from the NIST guidelines and is widely used throughout government and industry. You begin the flowchart at one of three locations, depending on what classification of information was on the media, and then walk through a series of decision points based on whether you plan to reuse the media and whether it will leave your organization. The flowchart then leads you to advice on either clearing, purging, or destroying the media.

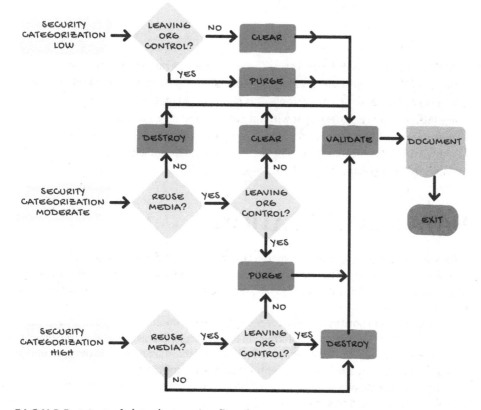

FIGURE 19.2 A data destruction flowchart

NOTE

If you don't want to handle data sanitization and destruction internally, third-party services are available that offer outsourced data destruction services.

Destroying Paper Records

You also should destroy paper records when they reach the end of their useful life. You have some different options at your disposal here:

▶ *Shredding* using a cross-cut shredder cuts them into very small pieces that are very difficult to reassemble.
▶ *Pulping* uses chemical processes to remove the ink from paper and return it to pulp form for recycling into new paper products.
▶ *Incineration* burns papers, although burning paper is less environmentally friendly because it creates carbon emissions, and, unlike pulping or shredding, burned paper can't be recycled.

EXAM TIP

While this process is described as a life cycle, it's important to note that the stages of the life cycle are not always followed in order and not all of them occur for every piece of data. For example, it is possible to create new data in memory, use it there, and then destroy it without ever storing it in a repository. Similarly, data might be permanently retained in active storage and never reach the archive or destroy stages. However, the life cycle is still a useful model for understanding the different stages of data life.

DATA CLASSIFICATION

Organizations use *classification* to help users understand the security requirements for handling different types of information. Information classification serves as the backbone of data governance efforts designed to help organizations provide appropriate protections for sensitive data.

Data classification policies describe the security levels of information used in an organization and the process for assigning information to a particular classification level. The different security categories, or classifications, used by an organization determine the appropriate storage, handling, and access requirements for classified information.

Security classifications are assigned based on both the sensitivity of information and the criticality of that information to the enterprise.

Classification Schemes

Classification schemes vary but all basically try to group information into high, medium, and low sensitivity levels and differentiate between public and private information.

For example, the military uses the following classification scheme to safeguard government data:

- ▶ Top Secret
- ▶ Secret
- ▶ Confidential
- ▶ Unclassified

A business, however, might use friendlier terms to accomplish the same goal, such as:

- ▶ Highly Sensitive
- ▶ Sensitive
- ▶ Internal
- ▶ Public

Businesses use these terms to describe how they will handle sensitive proprietary and customer data.

Organizations that deal with sensitive personal information should consider not only the impact on their organization if they lose control of that data but also the impact on their customers. For this reason, they should pay particular attention to safeguarding the following:

- ▶ Personally identifiable information (PII)
- ▶ Financial information, including credit card and bank account numbers
- ▶ Health information, especially records that are governed by HIPAA privacy and security standards

Data classification is extremely important because it is used as the basis for other data security decisions. For example, a company might require the use of strong encryption to protect Sensitive and Highly Sensitive information both at rest and in transit. This is an example of a data handling requirement.

Labeling

When an organization classifies information, it should also include *labeling* requirements that apply consistent markings to sensitive information. Using standard labeling practices ensures that users are able to consistently recognize sensitive information and handle it appropriately.

EXAM ESSENTIALS

▶ Data must be appropriately managed throughout its life cycle—from creation to destruction. This includes securely creating, storing, using, sharing, archiving, and ultimately destroying data when it's no longer necessary. The method of destruction should be secure, adhering to standards such as the NIST guidelines for media sanitization.

▶ Data classification is crucial for implementing appropriate security measures. Information should be categorized based on its sensitivity and criticality to the organization. Common classification schemes include military levels like Top Secret, Secret, Confidential, and Unclassified, and business-friendly terms such as Highly Sensitive, Sensitive, Internal, and Public. These categories determine the appropriate storage, handling, and access requirements for the data.

▶ Labeling of classified information should be standardized within an organization. This practice ensures that users can consistently recognize sensitive information and handle it correctly, thereby mitigating the risk of accidental data leaks or breaches.

Practice Question 1

An organization classifies its data into four categories: Public, Internal, Sensitive, and Highly Sensitive. Which of the following data would likely be classified as Highly Sensitive?

A. Press releases about new products
B. Internal policy documents
C. Customer credit card information
D. Employee cafeteria menu

Practice Question 2

You're a security officer at a corporation that has a strict data retention policy. One of the company servers reached its end-of-life and is being decommissioned. Which of the following actions is the most secure method to ensure that sensitive data on the server's hard drives is completely destroyed if you would like to potentially reuse the drives?

A. Overwriting the data
B. Formatting the drives
C. Degaussing the drives
D. Physically destroying the drives

Practice Question 1 Explanation

In this question, you need to identify which type of data would most likely be classified as Highly Sensitive. Press releases are public information and would fall under the Public category. Internal policy documents are typically Internal or Sensitive, depending on the content. Employee cafeteria menus are also typically classified as Public or Internal.

The only option that would likely be classified as Highly Sensitive is customer credit card information due to its nature and the significant impact that its disclosure could have on customers and the organization.

Correct Answer: C. Customer credit card information

Practice Question 2 Explanation

This question asks for the most secure method to ensure data is completely destroyed while still maintaining the potential for drive reuse.

Physically destroying the drives is the most secure method of data destruction, but it eliminates the possibility of reusing the drives, which disqualifies it as a viable answer.

Formatting the drives does not necessarily erase all data and could leave remnants that could potentially be recovered.

Degaussing is a process that demagnetizes the hard drives and can be quite effective, but it also makes the hard drives unusable for future purposes.

The most secure method of data destruction that still allows for hard drive reuse is overwriting the data, which ensures that the previous data is replaced with new data, making it difficult to recover the original data.

Correct Answer: A. Overwriting the data

CHAPTER 20

Logging and Monitoring
Objective 5.1 Understand Data Security

Logging and monitoring are at the heart of data security. As security events unfold, these two processes enable professionals to pinpoint activities, attribute actions to their origins, and maintain detailed records of user and system activity.

In this chapter, you'll learn about the third subobjective of CC objective 5.1. The remaining material for this objective is covered in Chapter 18, "Encryption," and Chapter 19, "Data Handling." The following subobjective is covered in this chapter:

▶ **Logging and monitoring security events**

LOGGING

Logs provide a treasure trove of information for security professionals, whether they're investigating an incident, troubleshooting a technical problem, or gathering evidence. When logging is configured properly, organizations can look at a specific event and achieve three important objectives:

1. They can determine who caused the event. That's a characteristic known as *accountability* or identity attribution. This attribution can be to a specific person, a computer's IP address, or a geographic location.
2. They can track down all other events related to the investigated event. That's a characteristic known as *traceability*.
3. They can provide clear documentation of those actions. That's *auditability*.

LOG MONITORING

If you're like most security professionals, you simply don't have the time to do a thorough job of reviewing logs. There are simply far too many log entries generated by systems, applications, network devices, and other event sources each day, and trudging through them would be tedious, mind-numbing work.

Fortunately, computers are very good at tedious work and most organizations now go beyond simple reporting and alerting mechanisms and apply artificial intelligence approaches to the problem of security log analysis.

Security information and event management (*SIEM*) systems have the following two major functions on an enterprise network:

1. They act as a central, secure collection point for log entries. Administrators configure all of their systems, network devices, and applications to send log records directly to the SIEM, and the SIEM stores them in a secure fashion where they are safe from unauthorized modification and available for analysis.
2. They apply artificial intelligence. This correlates all of those log entries to detect patterns of potentially malicious activity.

The great thing about a SIEM is that it has access to all of the log entries from across the organization. In a hierarchical organization, network engineers might have access to firewall logs; system engineers might have operating system logs; and application administrators might have application logs. This siloed approach means that attacks could go unnoticed if the signs of the attack are spread across multiple departments. Each administrator might see a piece of the puzzle but can't put the whole picture together.

The SIEM has all of the puzzle pieces and performs an activity known as *log correlation* to recognize combinations of activity that could indicate a security incident.

For example, an intrusion detection system might notice the unique signature of an attack in inbound network traffic, triggering an event within the SIEM that pulls together other information.

From there, a firewall might note an inbound connection to a web server from an unfriendly country.

The web server might report suspicious queries that include signs of a SQL injection attack.

The database server might report a large query from a web application that deviates from normal patterns, and a router might report a large flow of information from the database server to the Internet.

In isolation, each of these activities may seem innocuous, but when the SIEM puts those pieces together, a pattern of suspicious activity emerges.

EXAM ESSENTIALS

▶ Logs provide crucial insights into security events. They are instrumental in attributing activities to specific sources (accountability), finding all events related to a particular incident (traceability), and keeping accurate records for audit purposes (auditability).

▶ Security information and event management (SIEM) systems enhance log management by providing a centralized collection point for log entries, ensuring data integrity, and facilitating comprehensive analysis.

▶ SIEM systems leverage artificial intelligence to correlate log entries, detecting patterns that might signal malicious activities. This capability to recognize potential security incidents by correlating disparate pieces of information is a key benefit of using SIEMs.

Practice Question 1

You've just been assigned to improve the existing log management system in your organization. Which solution would best aid in centralizing, protecting, and analyzing your log entries?

A. DBMS
B. NIDS
C. SIEM
D. IAM

Practice Question 2

As a network security analyst, you are tasked with investigating an unusual surge in network traffic. You are looking for a way to connect the dots between different events and identify any potential security threats. Which attribute of effective logging is most useful for this task?

A. Accountability
B. Auditability
C. Availability
D. Traceability

Practice Question 1 Explanation

A database management system (DBMS) is used primarily to manage databases and is not specifically designed for centralized log management. An identity and access management (IAM) system is more focused on managing user identities and controlling their access to resources.

While a network intrusion detection system (NIDS) does analyze network traffic and create logs of suspicious activity, it doesn't have the capability to centralize and manage logs from various sources.

The security information and event management (SIEM) system, however, does exactly what the question requires. It provides centralized logging capabilities, securely stores logs, and employs advanced analytics to scrutinize log data for potential security incidents. So, the most suitable solution to improve the log management system in this scenario would be a SIEM system.

Correct Answer: C. SIEM

Practice Question 2 Explanation

When you are faced with an unusual event or a security incident, the ability to identify and follow all related events is crucial. This process is known as traceability. It helps analysts connect the dots between various events and provides a comprehensive view of an incident.

Accountability, or identity attribution, while important, is more about determining the origin or cause of an event, which isn't the primary need in this scenario.

Auditability refers to the documentation of events, which is valuable but not the main requirement for this situation.

Availability is more related to the accessibility and uptime of systems and data, and is not directly related to the investigation of security incidents.

Correct Answer: D. Traceability

CHAPTER 21

Configuration Management

Objective 5.2 Understand System Hardening

Configuration management is a key part of ensuring that systems and applications remain secure. It keeps track of how devices are set up, updates to software, and fixes for issues, called patches. We keep systems strong and secure for as long as they are in use by hardening them—actively managing and fixing weak spots.

In this chapter, you'll learn about CC objective 5.2. The following subobjective is covered in this chapter:

▶ **Configuration management (e.g., baselines, updates, patches)**

CONFIGURATION MANAGEMENT

Configuration management establishes and monitors the way that specific devices are set up. Configuration management tracks both operating system settings and the inventory of software installed on a device.

Baselines

Baselining is an important component of configuration management. A baseline is a snapshot of a system or application at a given point in time. It may be used to assess whether a system has changed outside of an approved change management process. System administrators can compare a running system to a baseline to identify all changes to the system, and then compare those changes to approved changes.

Version Control

Version control is also a critical component of change management programs, particularly in the area of software and script development. Versioning assigns each release of a piece of software an incrementing version number that can be used to identify any given copy. These numbers are frequently written as three-part decimals, with the first number representing the major version of the software, the second number representing the major update, and the third number representing minor updates.

Apple's iOS uses this scheme, along with many other software products. For example, iOS 16 is a major version of the iPhone operating system. When Apple periodically releases major updates to iOS, they add a second number to the version string, such as iOS 16.1. Then, if they make small updates to iOS 16.1 prior to the release of iOS 16.2, they add a third digit, such as iOS 16.1.1.

CONFIGURATION VULNERABILITIES

Configuration vulnerabilities can also have serious impacts on enterprise security. A few simple errors in a system configuration can result in very significant security vulnerabilities that an attacker can exploit to gain access to sensitive information or systems.

Default Configurations

One common mistake that IT staff often make is taking a system directly from a manufacturer and installing it on their network without modifying the default configuration. This is especially true in the case of devices that contain embedded computers but are not commonly managed as part of the enterprise IT infrastructure, such as copiers, building controllers, research equipment, and other devices that come directly from vendors. The default configurations on these devices can contain misconfigured firewalls with open ports and services, open permissions, guest accounts, default passwords, unsecured root accounts, or other serious security issues. IT staff should always verify the security of devices before connecting them to the network.

Weak Security Settings

System, application, and device configurations vary widely and can often be very complicated. Systems that are misconfigured or configured with weak security settings can be serious problems. Small errors can lead to significant security flaws that might allow an attacker to gain complete control of the device. IT professionals should always depend on documented security standards and configuration baselines to help them install systems in a secure manner.

Cryptographic Weaknesses

Cryptographic protocols are a common source of misconfigurations. If an administrator inadvertently configures weak cipher suites or weak protocol implementations on a device, all of the communications to and from that device might be subject to eavesdropping and tampering. The error can be as simple as clicking the wrong check box.

Administrators must also carefully manage encryption keys to ensure that they don't fall into the wrong hands. If a private key becomes known to a third party, that person can impersonate the key's legitimate owner, eavesdropping on communications, engaging in false communications, and creating false digital signatures.

Along those same lines, organizations must protect the issuance and use of digital certificates, ensuring that strong certificate management processes are in place to prevent the issuance of false certificates and protect the secret keys associated with digital certificates.

Patch and Update Management

Patch management ensures that systems and applications receive all of the security updates provided by manufacturers to correct known vulnerabilities. Remember that you need to patch many different components of your operating environment.

> **EXAM TIP**
>
> Operating system patches often get the most attention, but don't forget to patch applications and the firmware of devices used throughout your environment. A single unpatched device can provide the open gateway that an attacker needs to establish a foothold into your network.

Account Management

Finally, account management is an incredibly important task for security professionals. If an account is improperly configured with excess permissions, the user owning that account can use those extra privileges to cause damage. This can be intentional, in the case of a malicious insider, or it can be accidental when the user simply doesn't know what they are doing.

> **EXAM TIP**
>
> Remember the principle of least privilege. A user should only have the minimum set of permissions necessary to perform their job function.

EXAM ESSENTIALS

▶ Configuration management forms the basis of a secure IT environment. It involves documenting and controlling changes to hardware, software, and system setups, allowing for a stable and reliable operational environment.

▶ Baselines provide a snapshot of a system at a specific point in time. Comparing the current system state with its baseline can help you identify unauthorized or unexpected changes, enhancing security control.

▶ Updating and patching are integral parts of configuration management. Timely updates and patches fix known vulnerabilities, helping maintain the system's security integrity.

Practice Question 1

Your organization is implementing a new configuration management policy. As part of the new policy, what should be created for each system at a specific point in time in order to allow for a comparison of system changes in the future?

A. A system inventory
B. A baseline
C. An update history
D. A patch log

Practice Question 2

You are responsible for the security of an IoT environment and are concerned about correcting vulnerabilities by applying updates as quickly as possible. What aspect of configuration management most directly meets this goal?

A. Version control
B. Baselining
C. Patch management
D. System hardening

Practice Question 1 Explanation

A system inventory is a list of all the systems in an organization, but it doesn't include details about the systems' configurations at any point in time. Update histories and patch logs specifically track updates and patches to a system over time.

A baseline, however, captures the state of a system at a specific point in time. In the context of configuration management, it provides a point of comparison for future system states to identify any changes that have occurred.

Correct Answer: B. A baseline

Practice Question 2 Explanation

While all the options mentioned contribute to an overall secure environment, the one that directly addresses the concern of correcting vulnerabilities as quickly as possible is patch management.

Version control helps to keep track of changes made to software over time, which is essential in managing updates, but it doesn't address the quick correction of vulnerabilities. Baselining is a snapshot of a system at a certain point in time and is used to detect any changes to a system's state, but doesn't directly deal with vulnerability management.

System hardening involves reducing system vulnerabilities through measures like disabling unnecessary services and minimizing the number of system administrators, but it doesn't encompass the process of applying patches to fix known vulnerabilities.

Patch management, however, is the process of applying updates from manufacturers that fix known vulnerabilities. These patches help to secure systems against threats and are crucial in maintaining a secure IoT environment.

Correct Answer: C. Patch management

CHAPTER 22

Best Practice Security Policies

Objective 5.3
Understand Best Practice Security Policies

In Chapter 7, "Security Governance Processes," you learned about the different types of documents that are created as part of the security policy framework. This chapter discusses the content of those policies. Every organization will need a different set of security policies, but there are some common themes found in most organizations.

In this chapter, you'll learn about CC objective 5.3. The following subobjectives are covered in this chapter:

▶ **Data handling policy**
▶ **Password policy**
▶ **Acceptable Use Policy (AUP)**
▶ **Bring your own device (BYOD) policy**
▶ **Change management policy (e.g., documentation, approval, rollback)**
▶ **Privacy policy**

ACCEPTABLE USE POLICY

Most organizations have an *acceptable use policy (AUP)*. The purpose of the AUP is to describe what users are permitted to do with the organization's technology assets and what is prohibited. For example, AUPs often address whether personal use of computers and systems is permitted and how much personal use is considered acceptable. The AUP also normally contains language that tells users that they cannot attempt to access information or systems that they aren't authorized to access and the consequences that will occur if they violate the policy.

DATA HANDLING POLICY

Data handling policies describe the security controls and procedures that must be used to protect sensitive information. They define the types of information that the organization considers sensitive and describe how employees must safeguard digital and paper records that contain that sensitive information.

PASSWORD POLICY

Password policies cover the protection and use of passwords in the organization. Chapter 2, "Authentication and Authorization," discussed many of the requirements that organizations may put in place, such as password expiration, complexity, reuse, and length requirements. The password policy is where all of these requirements get documented.

BRING YOUR OWN DEVICE POLICY

Many organizations now allow employees to use their own smartphones, tablets, and computers to access company information. Organizations that allow this type of work should create a *bring your own device (BYOD)* policy that documents the requirements for using personal devices, the security controls that must be in place, and the types of information that can be processed.

PRIVACY POLICY

Privacy policies are an important way to communicate with employees, customers, and other individuals about what information the organization retains about them and the ways that they will store, process, transmit, and maintain that information. Privacy policies are often posted on an organization's website and can be enforced by national, international, state, and local authorities.

CHANGE MANAGEMENT POLICY

Finally, technology teams should have a *change management policy* that describes how changes are made in the organization. The change management policy should include the procedures that the team should follow for the documentation, approval, and implementation of any technology changes that will occur.

The change management process should also include the development of *rollback* plans that can restore the previous configuration if something goes wrong during or after the change. Strong change management procedures are one of the most important characteristics of a mature IT environment.

EXAM TIP

This chapter described many of the common security policies that you'll find in most organizations, but you should think of these as a starting point. Not every organization will need all of these policies, and it's likely that your organization will need policies not discussed here. Part of the role of security professionals is to help identify and create a set of security policies that is well-suited for their organization.

EXAM ESSENTIALS

▶ Acceptable use policies (AUPs) describe what users are allowed to do with an organization's technology assets, as well as the consequences of violations. They set boundaries for personal use and unauthorized access.

▶ Data handling policies lay out the security measures necessary for safeguarding sensitive information. They identify what type of information is deemed sensitive and prescribe procedures for its protection, both digitally and on paper.

▶ Password policies detail the requirements for password use within the organization, including aspects like expiration, complexity, and length.

▶ Bring your own device (BYOD) policies cater to organizations that allow personal devices for work purposes. They document security requirements, define what data can be processed, and establish the obligations when using personal devices for work.

▶ Privacy policies communicate how an organization handles personal data. They outline what data is collected and how it is stored, processed, and maintained.

▶ Change management policies guide how technological changes are made within an organization. They prescribe procedures for documenting, approving, and implementing changes, as well as rollback plans if things go wrong.

Practice Question 1

John, a new employee in your organization, prefers to use his personal smartphone for work-related tasks to maintain efficiency. As a security professional, you need to guide him according to the organization's rules and regulations. Which policy should John consult for the appropriate guidelines?

A. AUP
B. BYOD policy
C. Password policy
D. Change management policy

Practice Question 2

You're asked to draft a policy that clearly outlines how your organization handles, stores, and processes personal information about its customers. Which policy should you focus on?

A. AUP
B. Data handling policy
C. Privacy policy
D. Change management policy

Practice Question 1 Explanation

An acceptable use policy (AUP) outlines the acceptable behavior and usage of organizational resources, but it doesn't specifically provide guidance on using personal devices for work-related tasks. Similarly, a password policy provides guidelines on password creation, usage, and management, while a change management policy deals with procedures for technology changes within the organization.

A bring your own device (BYOD) policy provides guidelines on using personal devices, like smartphones, for work-related tasks. It specifies the required security controls, types of information that can be processed, and other rules for using personal devices in a work setting. Thus, John should consult the BYOD policy for guidance on using his personal smartphone for work.

Correct Answer: B. BYOD

Practice Question 2 Explanation

An acceptable use policy (AUP) typically outlines what behavior is acceptable when using the organization's IT systems and is not primarily focused on customer information. A data handling policy outlines the procedures for handling all types of sensitive information, but it doesn't necessarily focus specifically on personal information about customers. A change management policy deals with the procedures for making changes to the organization's technology and is not related to customer data.

A privacy policy, on the other hand, clearly outlines how an organization handles, stores, and processes personal information about its customers. It is usually posted on an organization's website and informs customers about what personal information is collected, how it is used, and the ways in which it is protected. Therefore, if you're asked to draft a policy related to the handling of personal customer information, the privacy policy would be the most appropriate focus.

Correct Answer: C. Privacy policy

CHAPTER 23

Security Awareness Training

Objective 5.4 Understand Security Awareness Training

Security awareness training is a crucial part of any cybersecurity strategy. It's an ongoing process that equips people to recognize and respond to threats, including social engineering, which manipulates individuals into divulging sensitive information. The training also emphasizes the importance of robust password protection. Understanding and adopting these measures can significantly improve an organization's defense against cyber threats, turning every individual into a proactive participant in maintaining security.

In this chapter, you'll learn about CC objective 5.4. The following subobjectives are covered in this chapter:

▶ **Purpose/concepts (e.g., social engineering, password protection)**
▶ **Importance**

SOCIAL ENGINEERING

Digital threats aren't the only issue facing information security professionals seeking to protect their organizations. Some of the most dangerous risks come from the human threat of *social engineering*. These are also some of the hardest threats to protect against.

Social engineering attacks use psychological tricks to manipulate people into performing an action or divulging sensitive information that undermines the organization's security. For example, an attacker posing as a help desk technician might use social engineering to trick a user into revealing their over the telephone. Social engineering attacks are the online version of running a con.

Social engineering attacks are successful for the following reasons:

- ▶ Authority and trust
- ▶ Intimidation
- ▶ Consensus and social proof
- ▶ Scarcity
- ▶ Urgency
- ▶ Familiarity and liking

Authority and Trust

Countless psychological experiments have shown that people will listen and defer to someone who is conveying an air of *authority*. Displaying outward signs of authority, such as dressing in a suit or simply having a look of distinguished age, creates a trust among those without such symbols.

Well-known hacker Kevin Mitnick describes an example of authority and trust in his book *The Art of Intrusion*. He tells of a social engineer who simply walked right into a casino security center and started issuing orders. Because he did so with an air of authority, the staff complied with his commands.

Intimidation

The second reason that social engineering works is *intimidation*. It's simply browbeating people into doing what you want by scaring them and threatening that something bad will happen to them and/or the organization.

A social engineer might call a help desk posing as an administrative assistant demanding that they reset the password on an executive's account. When the help desk asks to speak to the executive, the assistant might just start yelling, "Do you know how busy he is? He is going to be very angry if you don't just do this for me!" That's intimidation.

Consensus and Social Proof

The third social engineering tactic is *consensus and social proof*. When people don't know how to react in a situation, they often look to the behavior of others and follow their example. It's the herd mentality. This is what happens when someone is attacked in the street and nobody calls 911.

It's also how riots occur. Most normal people would never think of burning a car or looting a store. But once the crowd gets going and they see this behavior around them, many people join in.

Scarcity

The fourth tactic is *scarcity*: making people believe that if they don't act quickly, they will miss out. You see this each time a major consumer electronics company releases a new product. Why will people wait in line overnight just to get a new phone? Because they want to get one before they run out.

A social engineer might use scarcity to trick someone into allowing them to install equipment in an office. Perhaps they show up with a Wi-Fi router and say that they are upgrading the Wi-Fi in adjacent offices with a brand-new technology and had a leftover router. If the office staff would like, they can install it here. If they agree, they think they're getting early access to new technology, while the hacker is establishing a foothold on the network.

Urgency

Urgency is the fifth tactic of social engineers. With this tactic, the hacker creates a situation where people feel pressured to act quickly because time is running out.

For example, a hacker might show up at an office and say they are a network technician who is there to perform a critical repair and need access to a sensitive networking closet. When staff refuses to grant access, the hacker can say they have another appointment and can't waste time. If the staff member will open the door now, the hacker will perform the repair; otherwise, the network will probably go down, and they'll be out of luck.

Familiarity and Liking

The final tactic is simple: *familiarity and liking*. People want to say yes to someone they like. Social engineers will use flattery, false compliments, and fake relationships to get on a target's good side and influence their activities.

The best way to protect your organization against social engineering attacks is user education. Everyone in the organization must understand that social engineers use these tactics to gain sensitive information and be watchful for outsiders trying to use these tactics.

SECURITY EDUCATION

Security depends on the behavior of individuals. An intentional or accidental misstep by a single user can completely undermine many security controls, exposing an organization to unacceptable levels of risk. Security training programs help protect organizations against these risks.

Security education programs include the following two important components:

> ▶ *Security training* provides users with the detailed information they need to protect the organization's security. These may use a variety of delivery techniques, but the bottom line goal is to impart knowledge. Security training takes time and attention from students.

▶ *Security awareness* is meant to remind employees about the security lessons they've already learned. Unlike security training, it doesn't require time to sit down and learn new material. Instead, it uses posters, videos, email messages, and similar techniques to keep security top-of-mind for those who've already learned the core lessons.

Figure 23.1 shows an example of a security awareness poster.

Organizations can use a variety of different methods to deliver security training. This may include traditional classroom instruction, providing dedicated information security course material, or it might insert security content into existing programs, such as a new employee orientation program delivered by human resources. Students might also use online computer-based training providers to learn about information security, or attend classes offered by vendors. Whatever methods an organization uses, the goal is to impart security knowledge that employees can put into practice on the job.

> **EXAM TIP**
>
> Two very important topics to include in security education programs are defending against social engineering attacks and protecting passwords from unauthorized disclosure and use. In fact, both of these topics are specifically mentioned in the Certified in Cybersecurity exam objectives, so be sure to remember them!

While all users should receive some degree of security education, organizations should also customize training to meet specific role-based requirements. For example, employees handling credit card information should receive training on credit card security requirements. Human Resources team members should be trained on handling personally identifiable information. IT staffers need specialized skills to implement security controls. Training should be custom-tailored to an individual's role in the organization.

You'll also want to think about the frequency of your training efforts. You'll need to balance the time required to conduct training with the benefit of reminding users of their responsibilities. One approach used by many organizations is to conduct initial training whenever an employee joins the organization or assumes new job responsibilities, and then use annual refresher training to cover the same material and update users on new threats and controls. Awareness efforts throughout the year then keep this material fresh and top-of-mind.

> **EXAM TIP**
>
> The team responsible for providing security training should review materials on a regular basis to ensure that the content remains relevant. Changes in the security landscape and the organization's business may require updating the material to remain fresh and relevant.

FIGURE 23.1 **A security awareness poster**
Source: U.S. Department of Commerce

EXAM ESSENTIALS

▶ The main strategies that social engineers leverage—authority and trust, intimidation, consensus, scarcity, urgency, and familiarity—exploit human psychology to circumvent technical security controls. Training programs should emphasize the nature of these tactics, teaching employees to recognize and respond appropriately to potential social engineering attempts.

▶ Security training programs serve as the frontline defense in cybersecurity, empowering employees to recognize and prevent security incidents. Training efforts must continuously adapt to the evolving landscape of cyber threats, ensuring that employees remain informed about current risks and effective mitigation strategies.

▶ An effective training program covers a diverse array of topics, including general cybersecurity principles and role-specific responsibilities. Broad topics like social engineering and password protection form a foundation of awareness for all employees, while role-based training equips individuals with the specific knowledge and skills necessary to safeguard information within their unique job functions.

Practice Question 1

As a part of your company's security education program, you are asked to update the security training material. What is the main reason for keeping the training material updated?

A. To maintain the interest of the trainees
B. To ensure the training material remains relevant in an evolving threat landscape
C. To provide a refresher course for the employees
D. To cover more security topics in the training

Practice Question 2

A person contacts your help desk pretending to be a top executive's assistant, and demands immediate assistance in resetting the executive's password. The person warns that the executive will be very upset if their request isn't fulfilled promptly. Which social engineering tactic is being used?

A. Intimidation
B. Consensus and social proof
C. Familiarity and liking
D. Scarcity

Practice Question 1 Explanation

While maintaining interest, providing refresher courses, and covering more topics can be beneficial, the main reason for keeping training material updated is to ensure it remains relevant in an evolving threat landscape. The nature of cyber threats is constantly changing, and outdated training material might leave employees unprepared to deal with new types of attacks.

Correct Answer: B. To ensure the training material remains relevant in an evolving threat landscape

Practice Question 2 Explanation

The scenario presents a situation where a person posing as an executive's assistant leverages the potential of the executive's anger to compel the help desk to act quickly on their demand. This tactic, where a threat or fear is used to manipulate the victim into compliance, is known as intimidation. While elements of authority and trust could be present due to the impersonation of the executive's assistant, the primary manipulation here is the threat of the executive's displeasure.

Correct Answer: A. Intimidation

Index

ONLINE TEST BANK

To help you study for your Certified In Cybersecurity certification exam, register to gain one year of FREE access after activation to the online interactive test bank—included with your purchase of this book! All of the practice questions in this book are included in the online test bank so you can study in a timed and graded setting *plus* an additional practice exam, flashcards, and a searchable glossary.

REGISTER AND ACCESS THE ONLINE TEST BANK

To register your book and get access to the online test bank, follow these steps:

1. Go to www.wiley.com/go/sybextestprep. You'll see the **"How to Register Your Book for Online Access"** instructions.
2. "Click here to register" and then select your book from the list.
3. Complete the required registration information, including answering the security verification to prove book ownership. You will be emailed a pin code.
4. Follow the directions in the email or go to www.wiley.com/go/sybextestprep.
5. Find your book on that page and click the "Register or Login" link with it. Then enter the pin code you received and click the "Activate PIN" button.
6. On the Create an Account or Login page, enter your username and password, and click Login or, if you don't have an account already, create a new account.
7. At this point, you should be in the test bank site with your new test bank listed at the top of the page. If you do not see it there, please refresh the page or log out and log back in.